# THE EVERYTHING KIDS' GROSS COOKBOOK

Get your
hands dirty
in the kitchen
with these
yucky meals!

## Colleen Sell & Melinda Sell Frank

Adams Media
Avon, Massachusetts

**Editorial**

Publisher
  Gary M. Krebs
Director of Product Development
  Paula Munier
Managing Editor
  Laura M. Daly
Associate Copy Chief
  Sheila Zwiebel
Acquisitions Editor
  Kerry Smith
Development Editor
  Katie McDonough
Production Editor
  Casey Ebert

**Production**

Director of Manufacturing
  Susan Beale
Production Project Manager
  Michelle Roy Kelly
Prepress
  Erick DaCosta
  Matt LeBlanc
Senior Designer
  Colleen Cunningham
Interior Layout
  Heather Barrett
  Brewster Brownville
  Jennifer Oliveira
Cover Design
  Erin Alexander
  Stephanie Chrusz
  Frank Rivera

**Note:** All activities in this book should be performed with adult supervision. Likewise, common sense and care are essential to the conduct of any and all activities, whether described in this book or otherwise. Neither the author nor the publisher assumes any responsibility for any injuries or damages arising from any activities.

An Everything® Series Book.
Everything® and everything.com® are registered trademarks of F+W Publications, Inc.

Published by Adams Media, an F+W Publications Company
57 Littlefield Street
Avon, MA 02322
www.adamsmedia.com

ISBN-10: 1-59869-324-7
ISBN-13: 978-1-59869-324-9

**Library of Congress Cataloging-in-Publication Data**
available from the publisher.

Printed in the United States of America.

J I H G F E D C B A

This publication is designed to provide accurate and authoritative information with regard to the subject matter covered. It is sold with the understanding that the publisher is not engaged in rendering legal, accounting, or other professional advice. If legal advice or other expert assistance is required, the services of a competent professional person should be sought.
  —From a *Declaration of Principles* jointly adopted by a Committee of the American Bar Association and a Committee of Publishers and Associations

Many of the designations used by manufacturers and sellers to distinguish their product are claimed as trademarks. Where those designations appear in this book and Adams Media was aware of a trademark claim, the designations have been printed with initial capital letters.

Interior illustrations by Kurt Dobler and Melissa Sell Frank. Puzzles by Beth Blair.

*This book is available at quantity discounts for bulk purchases. For information, please call 1-800-289-0963.*

# Contents

# Introduction

Chances are you have some favorite places where you like to have fun where you live—from your bedroom to your backyard. But did you know that it's also tons of fun to hang out in the kitchen? No joke! Trying out new recipes, experimenting with ingredients, and playing with food can be so much fun. But this book takes fun in the kitchen one step further—it makes it gross! What's more fun than that?

This book shows you how to whip up your favorite foods in special ways that make them look gross but still taste great! You'll also find a whole bunch of gross jokes, riddles, trivia, games, and puzzles all through the book.

Of course, food is more than just fun and yum. It also has an important job to do—to give your body the nutrition it needs to grow and function properly. So in Chapter 1, you'll learn about healthy eating and drinking.

But don't worry! Food doesn't have to taste yucky to be good for you. All the recipes in this book make delicious stuff that kids actually like to eat and drink. And with an added dash of gross added to each recipe, you'll find yourself having more fun in the kitchen than you ever dreamed! You can eat almost all of your creations, with the exception of the fake slime, fake barf, and other gross gags in Chapter 9. Those are just for fun, not for eating!

Cooking isn't rocket science, but there are some tricks to it. Chapter 1 shows you how to follow recipes and how to use all the gadgets in the kitchen. Make sure to also check out the chef's secret cooking tips and the important cooking *Words to Know*, which you'll find all through the book.

Most of the concoctions in this cookbook are fairly quick and easy to make. For some, you'll need help from your parent or another adult. Of course, kids should always be supervised by an adult when cooking. Make sure to also follow all the Play It Safe notices posted throughout the book.

Have a great time getting gross!

Colleen Sell
Melinda Sell Frank

# Appliance Monsters

Follow the dots to find out which kitchen tools these gross creatures have gobbled up.

Chapter 1

An Icky
Introduction
to Cookery

Here's an example of a recipe that you'll see in the next chapter:

## Flies Floating in Bee Spit and Goatmeal

Rise and shine and suck down a bowl of mushy goatmeal (oatmeal) topped with flies (raisins) stuck in a glob of bee spit (honey) and swimming in cow juice (milk).

▶ Difficulty: *Medium* ▶ Serves 4

1 cup water
1 cup milk
1 cup rolled oats (not instant)
Salt
4 tablespoons honey
4 tablespoons raisins

1. In a large saucepan, combine the water, milk, oats, and a dash of salt.
2. Cook over medium heat—stirring occasionally—until the goatmeal begins to boil.
3. Reduce the heat to low and simmer for 2 to 3 minutes, stirring continuously, until the goatmeal thickens and gets goopy.

---

Are you ready to create deliciously gross grub? Good! Before you start cooking, though, there are some important terms, tools, and rules you need to know.

All of the recipes in this book are kid friendly, and you can do most of the stuff yourself. Of course, anytime you're preparing or cooking food, an adult should supervise and help you in the kitchen. This is especially important with recipes that involve using a sharp implement, such as a knife or grater, or an appliance, such as a blender, electric mixer, microwave, or stove.

In this chapter, you'll learn everything you need to know to get cooking in the kitchen. Read it and talk about it with your mom, dad, grandma, or whoever is your cooking assistant—and then let the slicing, dicing, simmering, and boiling begin!

## Recipe Decoder

A recipe is a set of instructions for preparing a certain type of food—for example, macaroni and cheese. You should always read the recipe all the way through before you do anything else to make sure you know which ingredients, tools, and steps you'll need to create your culinary concoction. The recipes in this book include the following information:

- Number of servings (or quantity) the recipe makes
- How difficult the recipe is to make
- Tools needed to make the recipe
- Ingredients needed to make the recipe, with amount of each ingredient specified (if applicable)
- Cooking or baking temperature (such as 350 degrees), if applicable
- Step-by-step instructions for making the recipe
- Amount of time to bake or cook, if applicable

# Tool Mess!

Welcome to Mr. Geezer's garage sale. He's going to be in deep doo-doo when Mrs. Geezer finds out he tossed her kitchen tools in a pile with his filthy-dirty garage tools. Find all the kitchen gadgets and color them in.

## Gear and Gadgets

Each recipe in this book includes a set of small pictures that lets you know which appliances, utensils, and other widgets you'll need to make the recipe. The following picture key tells you the name and meaning of each of the cool tools you'll be using:

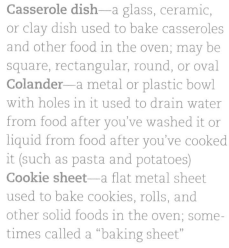

**Baking pan**—a square or rectangular pan made of glass or metal used for baking or roasting food in the oven

**Blender**—an electric appliance used for blending, chopping, or grinding foods

**Cake pan** (round)—a metal or glass pan used for baking a single layer of cake; may also be used for baking other foods

**Can opener**—an electric appliance or a manual tool (not pictured) used to open tin cans

**Casserole dish**—a glass, ceramic, or clay dish used to bake casseroles and other food in the oven; may be square, rectangular, round, or oval

**Colander**—a metal or plastic bowl with holes in it used to drain water from food after you've washed it or liquid from food after you've cooked it (such as pasta and potatoes)

**Cookie sheet**—a flat metal sheet used to bake cookies, rolls, and other solid foods in the oven; sometimes called a "baking sheet"

**Cutting board**—a wooden, glass, or hard plastic board used to cut, chop, dice, and slice foods

**Electric mixer**—an electric appliance used for mixing, blending, and whipping ingredients together

**Glass measuring cup**—a glass cup with a spout and measurements marked on the side used to measure liquid ingredients

**Grater**—a kitchen tool with a handle and a single flat surface or four different flat surfaces (shaped like a box) upon which are sharp-edged grooves used to grate, shred, mince, or slice foods, such as cheese

**Griddle**—a flat, square pan used to grill pancakes, French toast, sandwiches, hamburgers, and other food

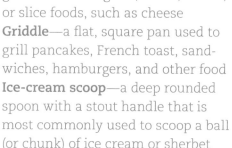

**Ice-cream scoop**—a deep rounded spoon with a stout handle that is most commonly used to scoop a ball (or chunk) of ice cream or sherbet out of a container

**Knife**—a utensil used to cut, chop, slice, and dice food; available in many shapes and sizes and with different edges, such as blunt (butter knife), serrated (ridges), and sharp

**Ladle**—a deep rounded spoon with a long handle used to scoop sauces, soups, and other liquids out of a pot, serving dish, or other container

**Measuring cup**—metal or plastic cups used to measure dry ingredients; usually come as a set of various sizes (¼ cup, ½ cup, ⅓ cup, ¾ cup, 1 cup, 2 cups) that are nested together

# An Icky Introduction to Cookery

 **Measuring spoons**—metal or plastic spoons used to measure liquid and dry ingredients; come as a set of various sizes (¼ tablespoon, ½ tablespoon, ⅓ cup, ¾ cup, 1 teaspoon, 1 tablespoon ) that are nested together

 **Microwave oven**—an electric appliance that uses electromagnetic (micro) waves to cook food, defrost food, and warm leftovers quickly

**Mixing bowl**—a large bowl used to mix together both dry and wet ingredients; available in several sizes

 **Muffin tin**—a metal or glass pan with small round cups used for baking muffins and cupcakes

**Oven mitt**—specially designed mitts and pads made with flame-retardant material used to hold hot pots, pans, dishes, and plates

**Pie pan**—a round, shallow, metal or glass baking dish with slanted sides used for baking pies and tarts; sometimes called a "pie plate"

**Pitcher**—a large glass, plastic, or metal container with a handle and a spout, used for serving water or cold drinks

**Plate**—a flat dish used to serve food

 **Potato masher**—a utensil with holes or thick wires on one end used to mash cooked potatoes, pumpkin, and other soft food to make it smooth

**Rolling pin**—a wooden, plastic, or metal roller with handles on each side used to flatten dough, such as for pie crust and sugar cookies

 **Saucepan**—a pot with a long handle used for cooking on top of the stove; comes in several sizes such as 1 quart, 2 quarts, or 3 quarts

 **Skillet**—a flat pan with sides and a long handle used for frying, stir-frying, and sautéing food in hot fat or oil

 **Spatula**—a flat metal, plastic, or rubber utensil with a long handle used to flip, lift, turn, or spread food

 **Stove**—a large gas or electric appliance used for cooking food; a stove that has burners for cooking on top and an oven for baking and broiling on the bottom is also called a "range," and sometimes the stove top and oven are two separate units that are built into the countertop and kitchen cabinets

**Vegetable peeler**—a sharp utensil shaped like a large keyhole used to peel the skin off of vegetables and fruits; also called a "potato peeler"

 **Toaster**—an electric appliance with two or four slots used for toasting bread, English muffins, and bagels

**Tongs**—a metal utensil with rounded pinchers (for grabbing food with) at the end of a long handle

**Whisk**—a metal utensil with a bunch of wires on the end used for mixing or whipping wet ingredients together

**Wooden spoon**—a big spoon used for mixing and stirring all kinds of food before cooking and while cooking; some have slats or holes in them

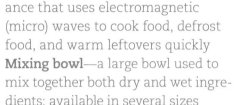

# Cooking Lingo

Every recipe uses certain words to specify how to prepare and cook food. Read the following descriptions of the most common cooking terms. Then ask your mom or dad or another adult to show you how to do each of these.

**Bake**—to cook food in the oven using heat from the bottom, usually putting the pan on the center or lower rack

**Batter**—a combination of wet and dry ingredients blended together to form a smooth or creamy mixture, such as the batter used to make cakes, brownies, cookies, and pancakes

**Beat**—to mix ingredients together by stirring very firmly and quickly, using a spoon, fork, whisk, or electric mixture

**Blend**—to mix foods together slowly and softly until the mixture is smooth

**Boil**—to heat liquid until it bubbles all over

**Broil**—to cook food in the oven using the heat source at the top, usually putting the pan on a top rack

**Brown**—to cook until a golden or brown crust forms on the food

**Chill**—to refrigerate food until it is cold

**Chop**—to cut food into small pieces with a knife, blender, or food processor

**Cool**—to let food sit at room temperature until it is cool enough to cut or eat

**Cream**—to mix ingredients together until they are smooth and creamy

**Dice**—to cut food into small squares of about the same size

**Drain**—to remove the liquid from food that has been cooked, defrosted, packaged, or stored

## Common Cooking Methods

**BAKE**          **BOIL**          **SIMMER**          **STIR-FRY**

**Fold**—to gently combine ingredients by lifting and turning ingredients from the top to the bottom until everything is mixed together

**Fry**—to cook or brown food in hot oil or fat in a skillet or deep-frying pan over high heat

**Grate**—to shred food into slivers with a grater, blender, or food processor

**Grease**—to coat a baking pan or baking dish with butter, margarine, oil, or shortening so food won't stick to the bottom while it is cooking (The coating can be applied by rubbing it on or spraying it from a can.)

**Knead**—to scrunch and turn dough until it's the right texture

**Mix**—to stir together two or more ingredients until they form one mixture (you can no longer see the different ingredients)

**Preheat**—to heat the oven or the pan on the stove to the temperature specified in the recipe before you start to cook the food in the oven or on the pan

**Sauté**—to cook food in a small amount of oil or liquid in a skillet on the stovetop over low to medium heat

**Simmer**—to cook over low heat until food almost boils

**Slice**—to cut food into long, thin pieces of about the same size

**Steam**—to cook food over boiling water so the steam cooks the food (The food doesn't touch the water or the bottom of the pan on the burner.)

**Stir**—to continuously turn and mix food with a spoon

**Stir-fry**—to cook food in a deep skillet and a small amount of oil over high heat while stirring constantly

**Whip**—to beat food very quickly with a fork, whisk, eggbeater, or electric mixer

# How to Measure Ingredients

Sometimes it's okay to use a little less or a little more of an ingredient. For instance, who cares if you put extra cheese on your pizza or half a cup rather than a whole cup of walnuts in your brownies? For many recipes, though, it's important to use the exact amount of each ingredient listed. Otherwise, you can end up with something that tastes like pigeon poop or looks like cow caca. Not enough yeast can make bread too chewy, and too much salt can make soup too salty, for example.

By the way, the cups and spoons you use to serve and eat with don't provide accurate measurements. When you need to measure precisely, make sure to use the right measuring tools and use them correctly by following these guidelines:

**Dry ingredients**—Fill the appropriate size of nested measuring spoon or measuring cup with the dry ingredient, such as flour, sugar, salt, or ground cinnamon. Then run a blunt knife over the top of the ingredient to "level" it evenly with the rim of the cup or spoon—unless the recipe calls for a "rounded" measurement, in which case you don't need to level.

**Solid ingredients**—Use nested measuring spoons and cups for soft ingredients, such as brown sugar, butter, margarine, peanut butter, jam, shortening, and shredded cheese. Instead of rounding or leveling the ingredient, gently pat it down with a spatula to remove air pockets. Do not pack the ingredient (similar to packing sand to make a sand castle) unless the recipe calls for it. Brown sugar is one of the few ingredients that is normally packed.

**Liquid ingredients**—Use a clear (glass is best) 1-cup or 2-cup measuring cup with a pour spout to measure liquids, such as milk, water, syrup, or soy sauce. Place the cup on a flat surface, bend down so that your eyes are level with the measurement marks, and fill to the specified level. Don't lift the cup up to your eye level to see whether it's on the mark.

Packaged ingredients sometimes come in different measurements than the ones used in the recipe. For instance, a recipe may call for 1 cup of yogurt, but the yogurt comes in a ½ pint carton. If you knew that 1 cup is equivalent to ½ pint, you could just dump the carton of yogurt into the recipe without having to put it in a measuring cup.

Knowing measurement equivalents will also come in handy if you can't find the size of measuring spoon or measuring cup called for in the recipe.

## CHEF'S SECRET:
### Measuring Success

Always measure ingredients over a paper towel or sheet of aluminum foil—never over the mixing bowl, casserole dish, or pot. That way, if you accidentally overfill the measuring spoon or cup, the ingredient won't spill over into the mix, and you'll always use exactly the right measurement.

One of the neat things about recipes is that you can make more or less food than the recipe calls for by reducing or increasing the amounts of all of the ingredients. Then, if you know measurement equivalents, you can use bigger measuring spoons or measuring cups rather than more of the same size. For example, if you wanted to use a recipe for 1 dozen cookies to make 2 dozen cookies, you would double (multiply by two) the amount of each ingredient. Let's say the original recipe calls for 2 tablespoons of vanilla. Double that amount is 4 tablespoons, which is equivalent to ¼ cup. So instead of filling the tablespoon four times, you could just fill a ¼ cup measuring cup one time.

**Weights and Measurements Equivalents**

| | | |
|---:|:---:|:---|
| dash/pinch | = | less than ⅛ teaspoon |
| 3 teaspoons | = | 1 tablespoon |
| 2 tablespoons | = | 1 fluid ounce |
| 4 tablespoons | = | ¼ cup |
| ⅓ cup | = | 5 tablespoons + 1 teaspoon |
| 1 cup | = | 16 tablespoons |
| 1 cup | = | ½ pint or 8 fluid ounces |
| 2 cups | = | 1 pint or 16 fluid ounces |
| 2 pints | = | 1 quart or 32 fluid ounces |
| 2 quarts | = | ¼ gallon or 64 fluid ounces |
| 4 quarts | = | 1 gallon |
| 4 ounces (dry) | = | ¼ pound |
| 8 ounces (dry) | = | ½ pound |
| 12 ounces (dry) | = | ¾ pound |
| 16 ounces (dry) | = | 1 pound |

## CHEF'S SECRET:
### Before You Begin Cooking

There are four simple things you can do to make your cooking experience easier:

**Plan ahead.** Make a shopping list of ingredients you'll need for the recipe you want to make.

**Read the recipe.** Make sure you understand every step and that you have all the ingredients and tools you'll need before you begin.

**Set up your cooking area.** Make sure you have a clean work area that you can reach. Set out all the ingredients and tools you'll need before you start.

**Protect your clothing with an apron or old shirt.** Make sure it fits snugly and won't drape on the food or stove.

**Measurement Abbreviations**

All of the measurement terms used in this book are spelled out, which makes it easier to follow the recipes. However, most packaging labels and many other cookbooks use measurement abbreviations. Here are the most common ones:

| | | |
|---:|:---:|:---|
| t. or tsp. | = | teaspoon |
| T. or Tbsp. | = | tablespoon |
| c. | = | cup |
| pt. | = | pint |
| qt. | = | quart |
| oz. | = | ounce |
| lb. | = | pound |

# Appendage-Saving Kitchen Safety

Did you know that most accidents are preventable? It's true. Follow these simple safety rules for preparing and cooking food to avoid accidents and injuries.

**Ask for help.** Your mom or dad or another adult should always supervise your kitchen activities. If something is difficult or scary for you—such as cutting something with a sharp knife or removing a hot dish from the oven—ask your adult kitchen helper to show you how to do it or do it for you.

**Keep clothing and hair out of the way.** Wear short sleeves or roll up long sleeves. Don't wear loose clothes that might brush against a hot burner, oven, or toaster or get caught in a blender or other equipment. Fasten back long hair.

### FREAKY FOOD FACT:
### Attack of the Gut Bugs

Most of the organisms that cause food poisoning need moisture, warmth, and a little time to multiply and destroy food. Some food-borne bacteria double in number every twenty minutes. Bacteria can make food go bad in two hours at temperatures above 40 degrees and in only one hour at temperatures above 90 degrees.

**Make sure you can reach the cooking surface.** If you need a boost, stand on a sturdy platform, such as a stepping stool; it's not safe to stand on a chair or sit on the counter.

**Use knives and other sharp utensils carefully.** Ask an adult for instructions or to cut, chop, slice, or grate the food for you. Always hold knives by the handle and always carry them with the sharp end pointed downward. Whenever possible, use a serrated dinner knife or plastic knife.

**Be careful using electrical appliances.** Keep them away from water. Make sure the cords are out of the way, so you won't trip or get tangled up in them. Never stick your hand or a utensil in a mixer, blender, toaster, or other appliance while it's running.

**Don't overfill cooking containers.** Some food expands when it cooks, and you don't want hot food to bubble or splatter out of the pot or pan and onto you or an open flame. Overfull containers also spill more easily when you are moving or lifting them.

**Never add water to hot oil, butter, or fat.** The water will make the oil pop and splatter, and it could burn you.

**Turn pot handles toward the rear or center of the stove.** This prevents someone from bumping into the handle and knocking over the pan—which makes a big mess and can cause burns.

**Use oven mitts and potholders to handle hot pots and dishes, or ask an adult to move it for you.** Never use dish towels, rags, or paper towels to lift or move a hot fork, spoon, lid, pan, bowl, cup, or dish. Never try to lift something that is too heavy for you to do easily.

**Keep flammable items away from hot burners.** Never put potholders, oven mitts, paper towels, or dishtowels on top of or close to the stove where they might catch on fire.

**Turn off the stove or oven before removing cooked food.** This reduces the risk of you getting burned. It's also a good idea to double-check the knobs to make sure they're all turned off when you're done cooking, before you leave the kitchen, which will prevent fires.

**Use heat-retardant utensils.** Metal handles can heat up and burn your hand, so always use wooden or plastic utensils or metal utensils with plastic handles to stir and turn food. Take the utensil out of the pan when you're done stirring or turning the food rather than leaving it in the pan while the food is cooking.

**Don't touch electrical appliances or outlets when your hands are wet.** To avoid shocking yourself, always dry your hands before plugging in or using an electrical kitchen gadget.

**Never put out a fire with water or by yourself.** If something catches fire, you should immediately ask an adult for help and step back so she can extinguish the fire and so you won't get burned! Small kitchen fires can usually be smothered with baking soda or a lid. If caught quickly, other kitchen fires can usually be put out with a fire extinguisher (a must-have for every kitchen).

**When you're cooking, never leave the kitchen to go do something else.** Leaving cooking food unattended is the leading cause of house fires.

**Clean up spills quickly.** If you accidentally spill something liquid or slippery (such as flour) on the floor, clean it up immediately so that no one slips and falls.

**Never use your fingers to lift up a can lid.** If the lid doesn't pop up after you open it, use a dull-edged knife or a spoon to pry the lid open.

**Focus on one thing at a time.** Take your time and follow the recipe step by step. The more you cook, the more your skill and confidence will build, and before you know it you'll be whipping out a whole meal. For now, take your time, concentrate, relax, and have fun.

## Battling Bacteria

When food isn't handled properly, it can become infested with harmful bacteria, which makes it toxic for people (and pets) to eat it. Eating spoiled food often causes flu-like symptoms—nausea, stomach cramps, vomiting, diarrhea, headache—which usually go away once your body has digested and pooped out the bacteria-infested gunk. But some food-borne bacteria can cause more serious problems and can even be life threatening. So it's really important to always follow these food safety rules:

**Use a clean kitchen and equipment.** Everything you touch and use while preparing and cooking food—including the countertop, bowls, measuring cup, spoons, pots, and appliances—should be clean. If there are dirty dishes near where you'll be working, wash them with warm soapy water or put them in the dishwasher or sink, away from where you'll be working. Clean surfaces often while cooking. Keep pets, toys, backpacks, and other stuff off the counter and table.

**Wash your hands.** Use warm water and soap to clean your hands before touching any food or cooking equipment and after touching any raw meat, poultry, fish, seafood, or eggs.

**Defrost frozen foods properly.** The safest way to defrost food is to place a dish under it and put it in the refrigerator overnight (for about 12 hours). Using the defrost setting on a microwave is okay too. Frozen food that is sealed in a plastic package or other leak-proof container can also be safely defrosted in a bowl of cold water. Never defrost food in warm water or on the counter.

**Use only fresh ingredients.** Check the expiration label on packaged foods. Before using fresh produce or leftovers, inspect it and smell it (but don't put your nose on it). If it smells stinky or looks putrid, don't use it. If in doubt, throw it out. Never taste raw meat, raw eggs, or any uncooked food or leftovers that are stinky, discolored, or moldy.

**Follow the safe food handling label.** All packaged foods have a label that tells you how to handle the food safely.

**Wash fresh fruits and vegetables.** Before eating or cooking raw produce, wash it thoroughly with cool water.

**Cook food completely.** Cook raw meat and poultry until it's no longer pink in the middle and no blood drains out when you poke it with a fork, or use a meat thermometer to cook it to the right temperature. Follow the recipe instructions for all other foods.

**Never reuse a kitchen tool without first washing it.** Don't use the same knife, cutting board, spoon, plate, or pan for cooked food that you did for raw food.

**Keep cold foods cool.** Refrigerated and frozen foods cannot be left out at room temperature for more than two hours. For picnics and barbeques, the limit is one hour, and it's best to keep cold foods in coolers until you're ready to eat them. Put unused refrigerated ingredients back in the refrigerator when you're done using them.

**Keep raw eggs and meats separate from other foods.** Keep uncooked eggs, meat, poultry, fish, and seafood at least 12 inches away from fruits, veggies, flour, sugar, oil, and other ingredients you're using in a recipe.

**Never sample uncooked or undercooked food made with eggs or meat.** This includes cookie dough, cake batter, brownie batter, and other recipes containing raw eggs. Raw eggs are a major source of salmonella bacteria, and raw meat is a major source of E. coli bacteria, which cause two of the worst types of food poisoning.

## FREAKY FOOD FACT:
### Good Gut Bacteria

Some of the bacteria in your body are supposed to be there. In fact, billions of these microscopic critters—enough to fill a 6-ounce mug—live in your colon (your large intestine) all the time, where they work hard to digest your food and turn the leftovers into poop. Every time you take a dump, you get rid of bacteria, both the good guys and the bad guys. Fortunately, your body usually produces new good bacteria as fast as you squeeze them out.

**Keep your hands out of your nose and mouth.** Don't pick your boogers, wipe your snot, bite your nails, or lick your fingers while cooking. This not only prevents bacteria from transferring from uncooked food to your body, it also prevents bacteria and viruses in your body from transferring to the food.

**Store leftovers quickly and correctly.** Seal all unused foods in an appropriate container or package. Put perishable food in the refrigerator or freezer as soon as possible. (Remember, no more than two hours at room temperature.)

**Heat leftovers until they're hot.** Stir while heating to make sure all of the food gets hot all the way through.

# Eat, Drink, and Be Healthy!

Making and eating good food is fun. It's also good for you. Food gives your body the nutrients it needs to grow, move, and think. Yes, even that big ball of twisty gray matter known as your brain needs food to develop and work properly. You don't need to eat gobs of food to be healthy. In fact, overeating can lead to obesity, which is bad for your health. To stay fit and to feel good, though, you need to eat enough of the right foods and limit the amount of not-so-good foods in your diet.

Scientists and doctors have researched the effects of diet on health, and we could write a book just about that. Lucky for us, the United States Department of Agriculture (more commonly known as the USDA) has put together a nifty food pyramid that makes it easy to under-stand how much of which kinds of foods to eat and drink to be fit and healthy. You've probably already heard about the food pyramid from school, so you'll just read about the basics here.

Most kids your age need at least 1,800 calories a day and sometimes more if they're very physically active. How many calories you consume is not nearly as important as how many servings of each food group you eat each day. The foods that appear at the top of the pyramid are the ones you need the least of, and the ones at the bottom are the ones you need the most of.

For most kids, a healthy diet is one that:

- Consists mainly of fruits, vegetables, whole grains, and fat-free or low-fat dairy products
- Includes some (not a large quantity of) lean meats, poultry, fish, eggs, beans, nuts, and legumes
- Is low in saturated fat, trans fat, cholesterol, salt, and refined sugars—in other words, junk food

### Grains: Six Servings

The major portion of your daily diet—at least six servings (equivalent to 6 ounces) should come from grains. At least half of your daily serving of grains (three per day) should come from whole grains.

For nutritional purposes, grains are divided into two groups: whole grains and refined (processed) grains. Whole grains contain the whole kernel of each grain. Refined grains have been milled, a manufacturing process that removes the bran and germ from the grain. Refining gives the grain a fine texture and extends its shelf life, but some of the grain's dietary fiber, iron, and vitamins are removed in the process. Check out this list of common whole-grain and refined grain foods:

| Whole Grain | Refined Grain |
| --- | --- |
| brown rice | couscous |
| oatmeal | crackers |
| popcorn | flour tortillas |
| whole-grain cereal | pasta |
| whole-grain cornbread | pita bread |
| whole-wheat bread | pretzels |
| whole-wheat tortillas | white bread |
| wild rice | white rice |

### Vegetables and Fruits: Five Servings

Fruits and vegetables add flavor, color, and variety to your diet. They also give you a slew of minerals, vitamins, and antioxidants (which help prevent and fight disease).

The USDA recommends three servings of veggies and two servings of fruits every day, but you can eat three servings of fruit and two servings of vegetables some days and still be healthy. That amounts to about 4 cups of fruits and veggies each day.

You can eat most fruits and veggies either raw or cooked (but always wash them first), and either fresh or preserved (but with little or no added sugars). There are hundreds of different types of fruits and veggies to choose from. It's best to eat more green and orange veggies than white veggies (which are higher in natural sugars). It's also better to get most of your fruit servings from the actual fruit rather than from fruit juice.

### Dairy: Two Servings

Dairy foods are a good source of calcium, vitamin D, and protein, which are all essential nutrients for your body. The dairy group includes milk and milk products such as cheese and yogurt, which usually come from cows and goats. People who are allergic to animal milk or who are vegetarians can use soy or another vegetable-based dairy substitute that is high in protein and calcium (which may be added).

The majority of the dairy products you consume should be low fat or fat free, and they should have little or no added sugar. Technically, ice cream

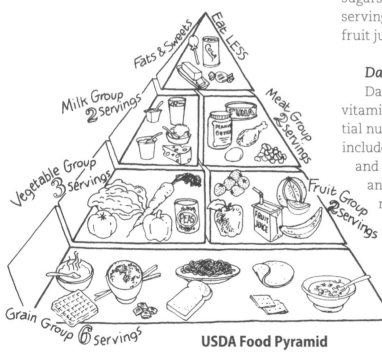

**USDA Food Pyramid**

in nutrients and high in fat, oil, sodium, and refined sugars—like candy, cheese puffs, cookies, donuts, French fries, potato chips, sugared cereals, and soft drinks. Though some of these foods are lip-smacking tasty, they don't help your body grow or stay healthy, and eating too much of this stuff for years and years can actually hurt your health.

There is no recommended daily serving for these foods because the USDA recommends eating very little of this type of junk food. The less saturated fat, trans fat, cholesterol, sugar, and salt (sodium) in your diet, the better it is for your health.

is a dairy product, but it is usually very high in fat and sugar, so you should limit the amount you eat and eat ice cream with as little fat and sugar as possible.

You need 3 cups (24 ounces) of milk per day. One cup of yogurt and 1½ ounces of cheese are each equivalent to one cup of milk.

### Meat and Beans: Two Servings

You should eat about 5 ounces of protein-rich foods each day. The USDA recommends eating a balanced mix of lean meat, poultry (chicken and turkey), eggs, fish, shellfish, beans, peas, nuts, and seeds. One ounce of meat, poultry, fish, and shellfish is equivalent to one egg, ½ ounce of nuts or seeds, ¼ cup of dried beans, or a tablespoon of peanut butter.

### Junk Food: Less Is Best

At the tip-top of the food pyramid is a food group labeled "fats and sweets." This group actually includes all foods that are low

# Trouble at the Table

Cross out the letters that appear twice vertically and horizontally. Then write the remaining letters in order (left to right, top row to bottom row) in the blank spaces below to reveal what troubles Tina.

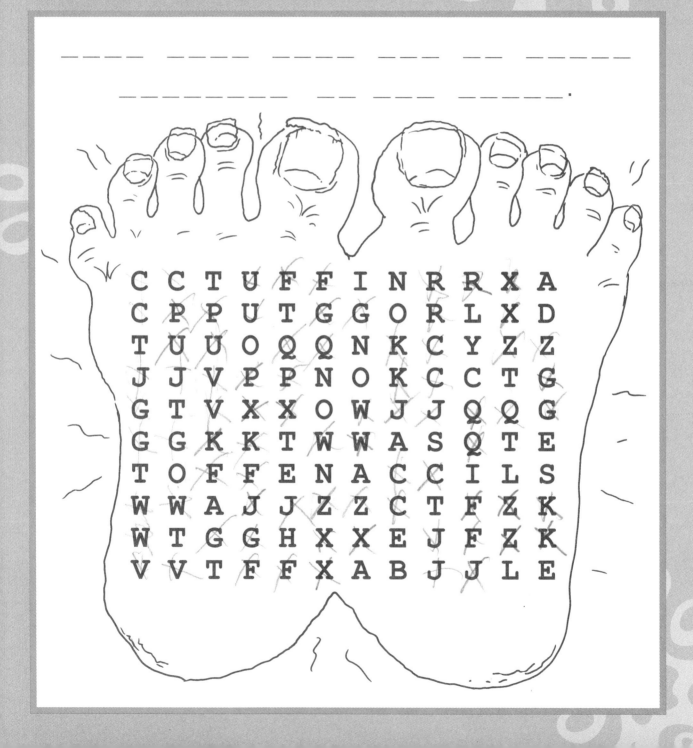

```
____ ____ ____ ___ __ _____

_____ __ ___ __ _____ .
```

```
C C T U F F I N R R X A
C P P U T G G O R L X D
T U U O Q Q N K C Y Z Z
J J V P P N O K C C T G
G T V X X O W J J Q Q G
G G K K T W W A S Q T E
T O F F E N A C C I L S
W W A J J Z Z C T F Z K
W T G G H X X E J F Z K
V V T F F X A B J J L E
```

# Chapter 2

# Bizarre
# Breakfast

# Squashed Gremlin Heads

These green pancake-heads are sticky, icky, and yummy!

▶ *Difficulty: Difficult*  ▶ *Makes 12 pancakes*

2 cups white or whole-wheat flour
⅓ cup sugar
1 teaspoon baking powder
½ teaspoon baking soda
½ teaspoon salt
2 large eggs, slightly beaten
2¼ cups buttermilk (or whole milk)
1 tablespoon vegetable oil (for the batter)
Green food coloring

Vegetable oil (for the pan)
Whipped butter
Blueberries (2 berries per pancake)
Sliced strawberries (one slice per pancake)
Bananas, cut in half and then sliced in half lengthwise (one slice per pancake)
Raspberry syrup (about 1 ounce per pancake)

1. In a large bowl, combine the flour, sugar, baking powder, baking soda, and salt. Dump the eggs, milk, and oil into the flour mixture. Stir until the ingredients are all mixed together but still a little lumpy. Add a drop or two of food coloring and stir gently just until the batter turns green.
2. Pour ½ tablespoon of oil onto the griddle. Heat the griddle over medium heat until a drop of water sizzles when you flick it on the pan. Using a large spoon (or a cup), drop about 2 tablespoons of pancake batter onto the hot skillet. Cook until the edges turn brown and the batter bubbles up.
3. Flip over the pancakes and cook until the other side is browned. Repeat steps 4 and 5 until you've used up all the batter, adding more oil to the pan as needed.
4. Put one pancake on each plate and use the butter and fruit to make a gremlin face on each pancake.

## CHEF'S SECRET:
### Is It Holey Yet?
You can tell a pancake is ready to turn over when the bubbles in the batter start to pop and the edges are firm. Carefully slide the spatula all the way under the pancake, lift the spatula straight up about 6 inches, and then quickly flip the spatula upside down and let the pancake fall onto the griddle (cooked side up).

Serve with warmed blood (raspberry syrup warmed for 20 seconds in the microwave). If you don't have or don't like red blood, you can pass around some warmed brown bile (maple syrup).

# Flies Floating in Bee Spit and Goatmeal

Rise and shine and suck down a bowl of mushy goatmeal (oatmeal) topped with flies (raisins) stuck in a glob of bee spit (honey) and swimming in cow juice (milk).

▶ *Difficulty: Medium* ▶ *Serves 4*

1 cup water
1 cup milk
1 cup rolled oats (not instant)
Salt
4 tablespoons honey
4 tablespoons raisins
Milk (optional)

1. In a large saucepan, combine the water, milk, oats, and a dash of salt.
2. Cook over medium heat, stirring occasionally until the oatmeal begins to boil.
3. Reduce the heat to low and simmer for 2 to 3 minutes, stirring continuously until the oatmeal thickens and gets goopy.
4. Turn off the stove and remove the pan from the burner.
5. Pour the oatmeal into four cereal bowls.
6. Put 1 rounded tablespoon of honey in the middle of each bowl of oatmeal.
7. Sprinkle 1 rounded tablespoon of raisins on each glob of honey.

🐛🐌 *If you like creamier oatmeal, pour a little milk (¼ to ½ cup) into the bowl and stir it up before adding the honey and raisins.*

**FREAKY FOOD FACT:**
**Pass the Bee Spit, Pilgrim**
Early European settlers brought honey bees to America more than 300 years ago. Not only did the pilgrims use honey (a.k.a. bee spit) in their food and drinks, they also used it as medicine and to make cement, furniture polish, and varnish.

# WORDS to KNOW

**breakfast** to "break" means to end, and a "fast" is when you go for a while without eating or drinking anything—such as all night while you're sleeping—so put these two words together and you get "what you eat to put an end to the nightly fast"

## CHEF'S SECRET:

Breakfast of Champions or Knuckleheads?

The best thing to eat for breakfast is:

**A.** Nothing
**B.** Donuts and soda pop
**C.** Cereal and chocolate milk
**D.** Ostrich-egg with boogies (green peppers), fungus (mushrooms), and mold (cheese); a slice of whole-grain toast; and a glass of orange juice

*D. Duh! Your body needs a helping of every food group at every meal, including breakfast. Only knuckleheads skip breakfast (answer A) or load up on nothing but sugars (answer B). Cereal is good for you, but only if it's made with whole grains and is not too sugary.*

# Chunky Crud Cakes

These chunky apple-cinnamon muffins might look like baked bird doo-doo, but they sure are delicious!

▸ *Difficulty: Medium* ▸ *Makes 12 muffins*

1½ cups flour
1 teaspoon cinnamon
1 teaspoon baking power
½ teaspoon baking soda
½ teaspoon salt
2 eggs

⅔ cup brown sugar
1½ cups chunky applesauce
6 tablespoons butter, melted
½ cup chopped walnuts or pecans,
   or unsalted sunflower seeds,
   shelled (optional)

1. Preheat oven to 375 degrees. Spray the muffin tin with cooking oil (or use paper liners).
2. In a large bowl, combine the flour, cinnamon, baking powder, baking soda, and salt.
3. In another bowl, whisk together the eggs and brown sugar. Stir in the applesauce and melted butter (cooled slightly).
4. Dump the wet mixture into the dry mixture. Use a wooden spoon to gently stir (don't beat) until creamy. Slowly stir in the nuts and/or seeds (if you like them and aren't allergic to them). Use an ice-cream scoop to drop the batter into the muffin tin.
5. Bake for 20 minutes. Remove from the oven and let cool.

*Eat warm or cooled, with or without butter on top. Wash down the crud cakes with a glass of milk.*

# Crusty Rusty Toast

This French toast, with its crusty (egg-dipped) and rust-colored (cinnamon) coating, looks like it came straight out of the junk yard. Add some oil (orange-maple syrup) and you're good to go gross.

▶ *Difficulty: Medium*  ▶ *Makes 8 slices*

2 large eggs (or 3 medium eggs)
⅓ cup milk
1 teaspoon cinnamon
2 tablespoons butter (or cooking spray)

8 slices bread
¼ cup orange juice
½ cup maple syrup

**CHEF'S SECRET:**
**Do You Vant to Suck Some Varm Tree Blood?**
To warm syrup for French toast, pancakes, or waffles, pour however much you think you'll need into a small pitcher (or measuring cup) and heat it in the microwave on low for 30 seconds. (Make sure the container is microwaveable.)

1. Whisk the eggs, milk, and cinnamon together in a bowl.
2. Melt 1 tablespoon of butter on the griddle over medium heat, or lightly coat the griddle with cooking spray and heat to a medium temperature.
3. Dip the bread into the egg mixture to coat one side, turn it over to coat the other side, and place the bread on the heated griddle. Do one slice of bread at a time (you should be able to fit 3 to 4 slices on the griddle).
4. Cook until golden brown on the bottom (about 2 minutes). Flip over and cook until golden brown on the other side. Remove from the griddle and place on a warmed plate.
5. Repeat steps 3 and 4 until all the bread slices are cooked. (You may need to add the other 1 tablespoon of butter or more cooking spray to the griddle.)
6. To prepare the orange-maple syrup: mix the orange juice with the maple syrup and warm in the microwave on low for 30 seconds.

*Chow down with a side of orange slices and a glass of milk. Napkins are optional—you can always just lick the syrup off your face.*

# Upchuckola

This concoction of dried upchuck (homemade granola) swimming in bile (smashed banana and brown-sugared milk) looks so close to the real thing it'll probably make your family gag. Nasty, yet tasty.

▶ *Difficulty: Medium*  ▶ *Serves 8*

½ cup honey
1 cup vegetable oil
3 cups rolled oats (not instant)
2 cups untoasted wheat germ
1 cup shredded coconut
1 cup dried milk
½ cup raisins
½ cup dried cranberries, blueberries, or cherries

¼ cup chopped walnuts
¼ cup slivered almonds
¼ cup shelled, unsalted sunflower seeds
Bananas, smashed
Brown sugar
Milk

1. Preheat oven to 350 degrees.
2. Spread the honey and oil in the bottom of a rectangular baking pan. Spread the oats and wheat germ over the wet mixture in the baking pan.
3. Bake 30 to 40 minutes, stirring every 5 minutes, until well toasted. Remove from oven and cool slightly (so you won't burn yourself).
4. Add the coconut, dried milk, raisins, dried fruit, nuts, and sunflower seeds to the pan and stir to mix everything all together.
5. Spoon the granola into serving bowls. Put about ½ cup of smashed banana on top of each bowl of granola.
6. In a creamer (small pitcher), stir the brown sugar into the milk until it is dissolved and the milk turns brownish. You'll need about 1 tablespoon of sugar and ½ cup of milk per bowl.

## PLAY IT SAFE:

What should you do before cooking or eating food?
A. Scrape the dog poop off your shoes.
B. Wash your hands.
C. Clean the dead bugs off the windshield of your family's car.

*B. Wash your hands, of course! You don't want poop, dead bugs, or any other kind of muck getting in the food you're about to eat.*

## FREAKY FOOD FACT:

The white part of a banana is:
A. A fruit
B. A vegetable
C. An herb
D. A berry

*D. A banana is actually a berry.*

Pour the bile (brown-sugared milk) over the upchuck (granola). Store the unused granola in a sealed plastic container or bag.

## Poop in a Scoop

Bananas and peanut butter for breakfast!

▸ *Difficulty: Easy*   ▸ *Serves 1*

1 whole-wheat hot dog bun
1 banana

1 tablespoon peanut butter
¼ cup (handful) raisins

1. Toast the hot dog bun.
2. Peel the banana and place it in the hot dog bun.
3. Use a butter knife to spread peanut butter over the banana until it's completely covered.
4. Sprinkle the poop pellets (raisins) over the top.

## Waffles Smothered in Pus and Scabs

Enjoy these nasty waffles smothered in pus (yogurt) and scabs (dried cranberries).

▸ *Difficulty: Easy*   ▸ *Makes 4 waffles*

4 frozen toaster waffles
1 (6-ounce) carton vanilla or custard yogurt
½ cup dried cranberries or cherries

1. Toast the waffles (in a toaster or toaster oven)
2. Drop a tablespoon of yogurt onto each waffle.
3. Sprinkle a handful of dried cranberries on top of the yogurt.

*For added grossness, squeeze some Hershey squirts (chocolate syrup) over your creation.*

A boy was frantically searching for a project he had made and wanted to take to school for show-and-tell. He suddenly remembered that he'd put it in a safe place the night before and dashed to the kitchen to retrieve it. He saw his sister sitting at the table eating a bowl of corn flakes. "Hey!" he said. "You found my scab collection!"

*Bet you didn't know scabs were so chewy and yummy, did you? These pus-and-scab waffles are great with a glass of pee (apple juice).*

## Brain Scramble

These scrambled eggs are gray, gooey (melted cheese), and smothered with blood (ketchup).

▶ *Difficulty: Medium*   ▶ *Serves 2*

4 eggs
¼ cup milk
¼ cup shredded jack cheese (or white cheddar)
1 drop blue food coloring
1 drop green food coloring
1 teaspoon salt
½ teaspoon pepper
2 tablespoons butter

1. In a large bowl, whisk together the eggs, milk, cheese, food coloring, salt, and pepper.
2. Melt the butter in a skillet over medium-low heat.
3. Pour the eggs into the heated skillet and cook until the eggs start to firm up. Then use a spatula to break up the eggs and turn them over. When the eggs are cooked all the way through (not runny), remove them from the pan and onto serving plates.

🐛 *Enjoy this brain scramble with blood (ketchup or Tabasco sauce) squirted on top.*

What do you get when you cross a pig with a centipede?

Bacon and legs!

# Rolled Boogers and Snot

Now you can have nose crud in a breakfast pudding made of toasted oats (dried mucus), white raisins (boogers), and custard (snot).

▸ *Difficulty: Easy*   ▸ *Serves 4*

1 cup plain yogurt (or vanilla or custard)
¾ cup prepared vanilla pudding (bought already made or made by your mom)
¼ cup white raisins
¾ cup rolled oats
2 tablespoons honey
3 bananas, peeled and smashed

1. In a large bowl, stir together the yogurt, vanilla pudding, and raisins. Set aside.
2. Heat a dry skillet over medium heat. Spread the oats across the bottom of the skillet and toast for about 1 minute.
3. Drizzle honey over the oats and stir as you continue cooking the mixture over medium heat until the oats are crispy on the edges. Remove the pan from the burner.
4. Spoon about half the oats into the bottom of 4 small bowls (or ice-cream sundae dishes). Keep some of the oats for topping.
5. Spread half of the smashed banana over the oats in the bowls. Pour a layer of pudding mixture over the banana layer in each bowl, using about half the pudding.
6. Put another layer of oats, then another layer of bananas, and then another layer of pudding into each bowl. Sprinkle the tops with the rest of the toasted oats.

*This breakfast pudding really does look like boogers and snot.*

> ## PLAY IT SAFE:
> Always use a long-handled cooking utensil to stir, turn over, or remove food in a pot or pan. Never cook with the small, short-handled forks and spoons you use to eat with. Cooking utensils have long handles for a reason—to prevent hot food and hot pots from burning you.

## Moldy Mushroom Caps

The mold (blackberry jam and cream cheese) all over these mushroom caps (English muffins) make them messy to eat and disgusting to look at. They taste so good you'll be drooling the whole time you're making them.

▶ *Difficulty: Easy*   ▶ *Serves 2*

2 English muffins
Blackberry (or black raspberry) jam
Cream cheese
Sesame seeds

1. Toast both halves of each of the English muffins. Put one muffin (two halves) on each plate.
2. Spread a thin layer of jam on top of each muffin half and then over the sides. Drop a glob of cream cheese in the middle of each muffin half. Use a butter knife to shape the cream cheese into a mound that is higher in the center than at the edges.
3. Dab little blobs of jam on top of the cream cheese mounds.
4. Sprinkle some sesame seeds on top of each muffin half.

🐛 *This recipe is also grossly great using bagels instead of English muffins and apricot jam rather than blackberry jam.*

### PLAY IT SAFE:

Never eat mushrooms you find outside, because some of them are poisonous. Only eat mushrooms you buy from the grocery store or the farmer's market.

Why do seagulls fly over the sea?

Because if they flew over the bay, they'd be bagels!

# Barfo Breakfast Tacos

When you scramble up this concoction, your family will think you've barfed this stuff up. The joke's on them, because this mess of eggs, ground sausage, and cheddar cheese stuffed into a soft taco is excelente (excellent).

▶ *Difficulty: Medium*   ▶ *Makes 4 tacos*

¼ pound ground chorizo (Mexican sausage)
4 eggs
¼ cup milk
½ teaspoon salt
Pepper (pinch)

1 tablespoon butter
¼ cup shredded cheddar cheese
4 soft tacos (corn)
Salsa to taste (optional)
Sour cream to taste (optional)

1. Brown the sausage in a skillet on medium heat, making sure it is cooked all the way through. Put the cooked sausage on a plate covered with a paper towel, cover, and set aside.
2. In a bowl, whisk together the eggs, milk, salt, and pepper.
3. Melt the butter in a skillet over medium-low heat. Dump the egg mixture into the pan. Cook until the edges firm up and then use the spatula to break up the eggs and turn them over; you'll probably have to do this a few times. As soon as the eggs are cooked through and there is no more runny stuff, remove them from the pan.
4. Mix the scrambled eggs, the cooked sausage, and the cheese together in a large bowl.
5. Warm the tacos in a microwave for 30 to 60 seconds.
6. Spoon the egg-sausage-and-cheese mixture into each taco. Add a dollop each of blood (salsa) and guts (sour cream).

*If you don't like chorizo or can't find it in the grocery store, you can use any kind of sausage you like—or you can use thin strips of ham. And remember, you can put anything in an egg scramble: diced green pepper, sliced mushrooms, chopped jalapeño (spicy pepper), bat's wings, frog's legs—you name it!*

# Can You Say Flatulence?

There must be fifty ways to say pppfffft! See if you can figure out these sixteen terms for the stinky puffs of air that lift you off your seat after you eat a huge plate of beans.

**Across**

1. Morning _____ (after lightning comes _____).
5. An ornery kid who smells bad.
7. Drop the _____ (another word for missile).
9. To tap a golf ball onto the green.
12. Break _____ (air that moves).
14. Two words that rhyme with one another and the naughty word for butt.
16. Trouser _____ (a type of horn in a brass band).

**Down**

1. The sound a horn makes.
2. When you pull the covers over your head and then let one rip.
3. Float an _____ (sky) _____ (a bread roll that's good with gravy).
4. Brown tracks left in your underwear.
6. Three words (3 letters, 3 letters, and 6 letters) that mean the same as "slice the cheddar."
8. _____ bongos (the cheeks you sit on).
10. Sphincter _____ (what the seven dwarfs did when they worked).
11. Rump _____ (rhymes with zipper).
13. Rhymes with heart.
15. _____ but deadly.

# Chapter 3

# What's for Lunch?

## Grilled Sneeze Sandwich

To totally gross out your parents, take the lid off this melted white cheese sandwich topped with sautéed green bell pepper and onion, then pretend to sneeze on it, put the lid back on, and take a big bite.

▶ **Difficulty: Medium**   ▶ **Makes 2 sandwiches**

2 teaspoons olive (or canola) oil
¼ cup green bell pepper, diced
¼ cup onion, diced

4 slices bread
Butter (or margarine)
4 slices jack cheese

1. Heat the oil in a sauté pan (or small, shallow skillet) over medium heat for about 1 minute. Sauté the green pepper and onion in the pan, stirring constantly, until the onion is translucent (you can see through it). Remove the cooked veggies from the pan and set aside.
2. Butter two slices of bread on one side. Put each slice, butter side down, on the griddle.
3. Lay a slice of cheese on top of each slice of bread.
4. Spread about 1 tablespoon of the sautéed peppers and onions over each slice of cheese.
5. Butter one side of two slices of bread. Put each slice, butter side up, on top of the sandwich.
6. Cook the sandwiches over medium heat until the bottom sides are golden brown. Flip over each sandwich and cook the other sides until golden brown. Turn off the skillet and remove the sandwiches from the griddle immediately.

CHEF'S SECRET:
No More Onion Tears
To keep your eyes from watering when you cut an onion, first peel the onion under cold water, chew gum while slicing the orb, and don't cut near the root. The cold water will reduce the amount of fumes rising from the onion, which are strongest near the root. Chewing gum will reduce the amount of tears produced by your tear ducts.

For extra grossness, you can mix in some blood (ketchup) with your boogers and snot (sautéed peppers and onions) and spread the mixture over the cheese before adding the top slice of bread and grilling the sandwich. You can also substitute white cheddar or Swiss cheese for jack cheese.

# Pickled Hambones

When cut into thick slices, these ham, cheese, and pickle rollups look like ham bones with gangrened marrow in the center—and they taste great.

▶ *Difficulty: Easy*   ▶ *Serves 4*

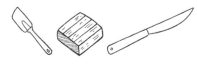

2 (10-inch) flour tortillas
Honey mustard
4 ounces cream cheese, softened
6 ounces thinly sliced ham
6 ounces American cheese, sliced
Pickles, dill or sweet (small)
Ketchup (optional)

1. Spread a thin layer of honey mustard on one side of each tortilla.
2. Spread a layer of cream cheese on each tortilla.
3. Place a layer of ham slices on each tortilla.
4. Place a layer of American cheese slices on each tortilla.
5. Place a row of pickles on one edge of each tortilla.
6. Roll the tortilla into a log and secure with toothpicks.
7. Using a blunt knife, cut the rollup into 1-inch slices.

🐛 *These pickled hambones are extra gross (and yummy) dipped in blood (ketchup)! If you don't like pickles in your rollup, try celery sticks or asparagus spears instead—or just stick with ham and cheese. After all, you're the chef.*

**CHEF'S SECRET:**
Which of these foods should be kept in a sealed, insulated container to prevent sickening bacteria from forming on it?
**A.** Boiled egg
**B.** Chicken noodle soup
**C.** Ham sandwich
**D.** Macaroni and cheese

*All of them! Boiled eggs and ham sandwiches should be kept cool. Chicken noodle soup and macaroni and cheese should be kept either hot (in a thermos) or chilled (in a sealed container until it's time to reheat them).*

What is red and green and goes 300 miles an hour?

A frog in a blender!

## Chopped Fingers

Want to enjoy a real fright fest? Serve these severed fingers (rolled turkey sandwiches) dipped in blood (ketchup) to your grandparents!

▶ *Difficulty: Easy*   ▶ *Makes 5 sandwiches*

5 slices thin-sliced bread
Butter (or margarine), soft or whipped
6 ounces sliced turkey (lunchmeat)

Cream cheese, softened
1 small red bell pepper
Ketchup

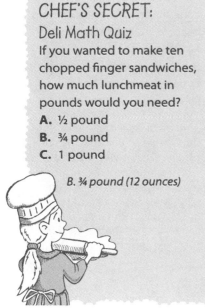

**CHEF'S SECRET:**
Deli Math Quiz
If you wanted to make ten chopped finger sandwiches, how much lunchmeat in pounds would you need?
**A.** ½ pound
**B.** ¾ pound
**C.** 1 pound

*B. ¾ pound (12 ounces)*

🐌🎗 *You can make these severed sandwiches using any kind of lunchmeat, or you can use peanut butter instead of lunchmeat and strawberry or raspberry jam instead of ketchup. However you stuff them, these severed fingers are ghoulishly delicious.*

1. With a rolling pin, gently flatten the bread slices. (Thin slices of lightweight white bread work best for this recipe.)
2. Carefully spread a very thin layer of soft butter or margarine on each slice of bread.
3. Place a slice of turkey on each slice of bread.
4. Roll up the sandwiches. If the seam won't stay together, spread a small amount of butter or soft cream cheese on the seam to make it stick together. Turn over each sandwich so that the seam is on the bottom.
5. Ask your adult helper to cut the red pepper into five pieces shaped like long finger nails, rounded on the top and squared on the bottom.
6. Spread a dab of cream cheese on the back of each red pepper fingernail (the side that's not shiny). Gently press the fingernail onto one end of each sandwich.
7. Place the sandwiches on a plate in the shape of a hand, with the fingers spread apart at the tips (fingernail sides) and touching at the other end. Squeeze (or pour) a pool of blood (ketchup) on the plate where the severed fingers meet (for dipping) and on the bottom edges of the fingers.

# Race to the Latrine

All the kids have a great time at Camp Wannagohomenow, except for when Chef Tootinscoot makes his infamous "leftover surprise meatloaf sandwich" for lunch. Then, as soon as the last chewy bite goes down, even the skunk has to hold his nose as the not-so-happy-campers make a mad dash to the poo-poo palace. Try to get from the mess hall to the outhouse before the rest of the campers do.

## Toe Jam Griddle

Imagine scraping the gunk out from between your toes, making a sandwich out of it, and then dipping the toe jam sandwich in eggs and frying it on a griddle. It would look a lot like this peanut butter and jelly French toast. Of course, it wouldn't taste quite the same—thank goodness!

▶ Difficulty: *Medium*   ▶ *Makes 8 slices*

4 tablespoons peanut butter
8 slices bread
4 tablespoons apricot jam (or jelly)
2 large eggs (or 3 medium eggs)
⅓ cup milk

2 tablespoons butter (or cooking spray)
4 teaspoons confectioners' sugar
Maple syrup (optional)

1. Spread peanut butter on four slices of bread. Spread jam on the other four slices of bread. Put each peanut butter slice on top of a jam slice to make four PB&J sandwiches.
2. Whisk the eggs and milk together in a large bowl.
3. Melt 1 tablespoon of butter on the griddle over medium heat, or lightly coat the griddle with cooking spray and heat to a medium temperature. Dip one sandwich into the egg mixture to coat one side, turn it over to coat the other side, and place the sandwich on the heated griddle.
4. Cook until golden brown on the bottom (about 2 minutes). Flip over and cook until golden brown on the other side. Remove from the griddle and place on a warmed plate.
5. Repeat steps 6 and 7 until all the sandwiches are cooked. (You may need to add the other 1 tablespoon of butter or more cooking spray to the griddle.) Sprinkle confectioners' sugar on top of each slice of French toast (about ½ teaspoon per slice).

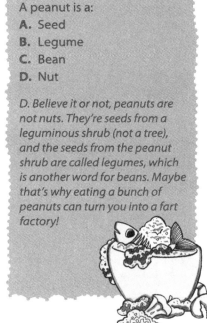

FREAKY FOOD FACT:

A peanut is a:

A. Seed
B. Legume
C. Bean
D. Nut

*D. Believe it or not, peanuts are not nuts. They're seeds from a leguminous shrub (not a tree), and the seeds from the peanut shrub are called legumes, which is another word for beans. Maybe that's why eating a bunch of peanuts can turn you into a fart factory!*

*Serve immediately, while the toast is still warm, with or without maple syrup.*

# Boiled Octopus

These juicy hot dogs have eight legs, just like slimy octopuses. They're delicious served open-faced on a bed of seaweed (pickle relish), creamy fish caca (mustard), and shark's blood (ketchup).

▶ *Difficulty: Medium*  ▶ *Serves 4*

4 hot dogs
4 hot dog buns
4 teaspoons sweet relish (optional)

Ketchup (optional)
Mustard (optional)

1. Starting at about 1 inch from the end of a hot dog, cut a slit down the length of the hot dog. Turn the hot dog and make another slit about ½ inch to the left or right of the first slit. Keep making slits until the hot dog has eight "legs." Do the same thing for all four hot dogs. (Remember to leave a 1-inch "head" on one end of each hot dog.)
2. Spread open the hot dog buns and place them on plates.
3. Spread each bun with your favorite condiments: pickled seaweed (pickle relish), shark blood (ketchup), or creamy fish caca (mustard).
4. Fill a saucepan about three-quarters of the way with cool water. Bring to a boil over medium-high heat.
5. Reduce the heat to simmer. Use the tongs to carefully place the hot dogs in the boiling water. Cover and cook 3 to 5 minutes. (While the hot dogs are cooking, wash the tongs or grab clean ones.)
6. Remove each hot dog from the pot, gently grabbing it by the 1-inch "head" with the tongs, and place the hot dogs on a plate to cool for a minute or two. Arrange each octopus dog so that the "legs" spread out over the bun like an octopus, with the head sticking up in the center.

**PLAY IT SAFE:**
Always turn off the burner before removing food from a pot or pan, and always turn off the oven before removing a pan or dish from the oven.

🐌 *You'll need a fork and a blunt knife to eat your hot dogs open-faced (with the bun opened up), and it's more gross and fun that way. If you want though, you can just stuff the legs into the bun, close the bun, and gobble it up.*

## Zit-Face Pizza

Every kid loves pizza! It's even better when you serve your friends these mini pizzas that look like pimply faces with oozing pus and greenheads just waiting to be popped!

▶ *Difficulty: Easy* ▶ *Serves 4*

What do you get when you eat a prune pizza?

Pizzarrhea!

4 English muffins, split
1 (8-ounce) jar (or can) pizza or spaghetti sauce
1 cup shredded mozzarella cheese
Black olives, sliced
1 (8-ounce) can pineapple chunks
1 red bell pepper, cut in strips
¼ cup frozen peas

**FREAKY FOOD FACT:**
Pizza My Heartland
Americans eat 100 acres of pizza a day!

1. Lightly toast the muffins in a toaster (or oven toaster).
2. Preheat oven to 400 degrees.
3. Spread 1 rounded tablespoon of pizza sauce on each muffin half. Sprinkle each muffin with mozzarella cheese.
4. To make the eyes on the pizza face, place 2 olive slices near the top of each muffin half. To make the nose, place a pineapple chunk in the center of each muffin half. To make the mouth, place a slice of red bell pepper at the bottom of each muffin half. (You can slice the pepper with a blunt knife yourself or ask your adult helper to do it for you with a sharp knife.)
5. Place a few green peas on the cheeks of each muffin face.
6. Place the muffins on a cookie sheet and bake 5 to 6 minutes, until the cheese melts. Remove muffins from cookie sheet immediately.

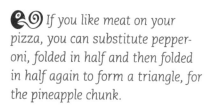 *If you like meat on your pizza, you can substitute pepperoni, folded in half and then folded in half again to form a triangle, for the pineapple chunk.*

# Cheesy Moose Veins

Tickle your funny bone with this macaroni and cheese made with moose veins (elbow macaroni dyed blue).

▸ *Difficulty: Hard*   ▸ *Serves 4*

3 cups cheddar cheese, grated
2 drops blue food coloring
8 ounces elbow macaroni
2 tablespoons vegetable oil
2 tablespoons flour

3 cups milk
1 teaspoon salt
¼ teaspoon black pepper
Cooking oil spray
½ cup unseasoned bread crumbs

1. Grate the cheese. Divide the grated cheese into two portions—2 cups and 1 cup—and set aside.
2. Preheat oven to 350 degrees.
3. Fill a 2-quart saucepan three-quarters of the way with cool water (about 6 cups). Add the blue food coloring. Bring to a boil over medium-high heat.
4. Reduce the heat to medium and cook the macaroni in the boiling blue water until tender, about 10 minutes, stirring occasionally. Remove from heat, drain, and set aside to cool.
5. In a saucepan over moderate heat, whisk together the oil and flour. Cook for 5 minutes, stirring constantly. Gradually whisk in the milk. Reduce the heat to low. Add salt and pepper. Cook 1 to 2 minutes, stirring constantly. Fold in 2 cups of the cheese. Remove the pot from the heat
7. Lightly coat a 2-quart baking dish with cooking spray (or butter). Pour the cooked macaroni and the cheese sauce into the baking dish, and mix together with a wooden spoon.
8. Spread the remaining 1 cup of grated cheese and the bread crumbs over the macaroni. Bake about 30 minutes, until the casserole is bubbly and a golden crust forms on top.

## CHEF'S SECRET:
### No More Boil Overs
To help prevent pasta, rice, or potatoes from boiling over:
1. Butter or oil the rim of the pot before adding water.
2. Fill the pot no more than three-quarters of the way full.
3. Bring it to a boil slowly (never with the burner on full blast) and watch your pot.

*For an added dose of gross and flavor, squirt some blood (ketchup) on top of your heaping helping of cheesy, chopped moose veins.*

## Fish-Eye Tacos

Here's an idea: Put two of these easy-to-make tuna eye-balls in a taco shell, hand the taco to somebody you love to gross out, and say, "Here's lookin' at you, tuna breath!"

▸ *Difficulty: Easy*   ▸ *Makes 8 tacos*

2 (6-ounce) cans tuna
1 large mild green chili pepper or bell pepper, chopped (optional)
2 tablespoons onion, chopped
½ cup mayonnaise
2 cups lettuce, shredded
2 medium tomatoes, diced

2 cups jack or cheddar cheese, grated
8 hard taco shells
¼ cup sour cream
1 (2¼-ounce) can black olives, pitted and sliced

1. Open the cans of tuna, drain the water or oil completely, and spoon the chunks or flakes of tuna into a large bowl.
2. Chop the chili pepper and the onion (or ask your adult helper to do it) and put them in the bowl with the tuna.
3. Add the mayonnaise and use a wooden spoon to blend it in with the tuna and chopped onion and chili pepper.
4. Shred the lettuce. Chop the tomatoes. Grate the cheese. (Or ask your adult helper to do these things for you.) Use two wooden spoons to mix the lettuce, tomatoes, and cheese together in a bowl.
5. Use an ice-cream scoop to place two tuna balls in each taco shell. Place the tacos on a plate.
6. Put a dollop (about 1 teaspoon) of sour cream on each tuna ball, and then put an olive slice on the sour cream to complete each eyeball.

### CHEF'S SECRET:
### Got Milk?
The best way to neutralize capsaicin, the stuff in chili peppers that makes your mouth burn, is with casein, a protein found in milk. So, if a spicy pepper sets your tongue on fire, drink a cool glass of cow juice.

*If you don't like chili peppers, substitute 1½ tablespoons of pickle relish (sweet) or 1½ tablespoons of chopped celery (salty). Ole!*

# Bloody Maggot Soup

Ah, there's nothing like a warm bowl of blood swimming with maggots (tomato-rice soup) on a cold winter's day. Schlurp!

▶ *Difficulty: Hard*   ▶ *Serves 6*

1¼ cups cooked white rice
⅓ cup onion, diced
1 clove garlic, minced
1½ tablespoons butter
3 tablespoons flour
1 (28-ounce) can tomatoes, diced, in juice

2 cups chicken or vegetable stock (broth)
½ cup orange juice
¼ teaspoon salt
⅛ teaspoon sugar
⅛ teaspoon ground paprika or cayenne pepper

1. Prepare the white rice according to the directions on the package. Set aside.
2. Dice the onion and mince the garlic (or ask your adult helper to do it). In a large (3-quart) saucepan or soup pot, melt the butter in a skillet over medium heat. Add onions and garlic, and cook until tender but not browned.
3. Stir the flour into the pot and cook for 2 minutes.
4. Stir in the tomatoes, broth, and orange juice. Bring to a boil, and then reduce the heat to low and simmer for 15 minutes, stirring every 4 to 6 minutes.
5. Remove from heat and stir in the salt, sugar, paprika, and ½ cup rice.
6. Puree the soup in a blender or food processor.
7. Pour the soup back into the pot. Stir in the remaining rice and cook over medium-low heat for 5 to 10 minutes.

**puree** to mix and mash food until it is the consistency of baby food

The frog motioned the waiter to his table in the restaurant and asked, "Why isn't there a fly in my soup?"

🌀 *For an extra crunch of gross, toss a handful of dried bones (croutons) on top of each steaming bowl of this bloody maggot soup.*

## Pick 'Em and Dip 'Em

Here's a chance to mix and match your favorite finger foods and then pair them up with your favorite dip: slimy snot (honey mustard), chunky monkey spit (sweet and sour sauce), horsey squirts (barbecue sauce), bloody nose blow (salsa), or pigeon poop (ranch dressing).

▶ *Difficulty: Easy*  ▶ *Serves 1*

1 cup fresh vegetables (sliced or bite-sized chunks of two or three veggies of your choice: carrots, celery, broccoli, jicama, sugar peas, bell peppers, cherry tomatoes, cucumber, pickles, olives, garbanzo beans, or soybeans)
1 or 2 slices of lunchmeat (turkey, ham, bologna, roast beef, chicken)
1 or 2 slices of cheese (American, Swiss, cheddar, jack)
3 or 4 crackers, pretzels, or other crunchy snack
4 tablespoons dipping sauce (any kind)

1. Wash and dry the veggies. Cut them into strips or chunks, if you want. Put them on a plate.
2. Put the lunchmeat and cheese slices on the plate. If you want to eat the lunchmeat and cheese on crackers, cut each slice into four pieces.
3. Put the crackers, pretzels, chips, or bread slices on the plate.
4. Put the dip in a small bowl or on the side of the plate.

**PLAY IT SAFE:**

Always wash fresh produce (fruits, vegetables, beans, and legumes) thoroughly with cool water before eating them raw or cooking them.

**FREAKY FOOD FACT:**

Which of these vegetables is actually a fruit?
**A.** Avocado
**B.** Eggplant
**C.** Olive
**D.** Tomato

*They're all fruits!*

When your friends come over for a sleepover or birthday party, you can make a whole platter full of a whole bunch of different finger foods and all five of these dips!

# Flat Worm and Seaweed Soup

This chicken noodle soup will help stifle your sniffles when you've got a cold. Of course, you can enjoy the flat worms (egg noodles) slithering down your gullet anytime.

▸ *Difficulty: Hard*  ▸ *Serves 4 to 6*

**CHEF'S SECRET:**
To Sop Up Soup Grease
Place a leaf of lettuce on top of soup while it's cooking. The lettuce will absorb grease that rises to the top. Remove the grease-soaked lettuce and discard it.

1 cup fresh baby spinach
2 tablespoons olive oil
1 clove garlic, minced
2 cups carrots, chopped
2 cups celery, chopped
½ cup green onions, chopped
1 teaspoon dried tarragon

1 teaspoon salt
1 teaspoon pepper
2 pounds chicken drumsticks or thighs
6 cups low-sodium chicken broth
8 ounces wide egg noodles (half of a 1-pound package)

1. Wash the spinach well. Remove the stems. Set aside.
2. In a large soup pot, heat the olive oil over medium-low heat. Add the minced garlic and then the carrots, celery, and onion. Cook until the vegetables are soft.
3. Stir in the tarragon, salt, and pepper. Add the chicken and broth. Increase the heat to medium high and bring to a boil.
4. Reduce heat to low, cover, and simmer for 30 minutes. Turn off the burner.
5. Remove the chicken from the pot and cool on a platter for 10 minutes. Pull the chicken from the bone and skin with a fork. Cut the chicken into pieces of about the same size (1-inch thick). Throw away the bones and skin.
6. Return the soup to a boil. Add the egg noodles, reduce the heat to medium, and cook for 6 minutes. Add the chicken pieces to the soup and cook for 2 minutes. Add the spinach and cook until the spinach wilts, 2 to 3 minutes.

*Ladle into bowls while your worms are still hot. Sprinkle with shredded Parmesan cheese. If you like a thinner soup, add more (1 or 2 cups) canned broth or water in step 3.*

## Spit-Wad Sandwiches

These peanut butter and spit-wad (mini marshmallow) sandwiches are easy to make and to pack in your school lunch.

▶ *Difficult: Easy*   ▶ *Makes 1 sandwich*

2 slices bread (any kind)
2 tablespoons peanut butter
1 handful mini marshmallows

1. Spread each slice of bread with peanut butter.
2. Rip the marshmallows in two and stick them all over the peanut butter on one slice of bread.
3. Put the two slices of bread together, with the peanut butter sides facing one another.

🐌 *Your friends will love these too. And they'll give you and your pals plenty of energy to have a real spit-wad fight!*

What do spiders like to order at a fast-food restaurant?

Burgers and flies!

## PLAY IT SAFE:

Never pound or tap on a glass jar with a knife or other object to try to loosen a stubborn lid, and don't bang the jar on the counter or anything else. If you're having trouble opening the lid on a glass jar or bottle, try running it under cold water, then dry it off completely and try again. If that doesn't work, ask an adult to open it for you.

# Fart Fuel

Gas up with these lip-smacking, finger-licking beans and weenies! You'll have energy—and air—to spare.

▶ *Difficulty: Easy* ▶ *Serves 4 to 6*

6 ounces mini bratwursts
2 (16-ounce) cans plain baked beans
1 tablespoon Worcestershire sauce
¼ cup brown sugar
2 tablespoons barbeque sauce (or prepared chili sauce)
1 tablespoon teriyaki sauce

1. Put the mini bratwursts in a separate saucepan and add water to completely cover the bratwursts. Cover and cook over medium heat for 8 to 10 minutes.
2. Remove the bratwursts from the heat. Drain the liquid from the meat and set aside.
3. Open the can of beans and empty into a saucepan.
4. Stir the Worcestershire sauce, brown sugar, barbecue sauce, and teriyaki sauce in with the beans. Cook over low heat for 5 minutes, stirring occasionally.
5. Add the cooked bratwursts to the beans. Cook another 5 minutes or until the mixture is completely heated through, stirring occasionally.

*A bowl or two of these go down nice and easy. Then, just sit back and let the butt bongos begin!*

CHEF'S SECRET:
Defuse a Stink Bomb
To remove gas-producing sugars from dried beans:
1. Soak beans overnight in cool water.
2. Rinse beans several times before cooking.
3. Never cook beans in the same water you soaked them in.

What can you make from baked beans and onions?

Tear gas!

# Barf-A-Rhyme

Sometimes when you eat something totally gross—like rotten eggs or pickled Brussels sprouts—your stomach says, "No way, Jose!" and spews it right back out.

Write the rhyming words that mean the same thing as "toss your cookies."

scarf        _ _ _ _

comet      _ _ _ _ _

twirl        _ _ _ _

snow       _ _ _ _

woodchuck   _ _ _ _ _ _ _ _

sleeve      _ _ _ _ _

duke        _ _ _ _

shelf        _ _ _ _

use hunch (2 words)   _ _ _ _   _ _ _ _ _

fetch        _ _ _ _ _

chin up (2 words)   _ _ _ _ _   _ _

hesitate    _ _ _ _ _ _ _ _ _

# Chapter 4

# Wacky Snacks

## Bugs on a Weed

When you bite into a stalk of crunchy celery stuffed with creamy peanut butter and chewy raisins, just close your eyes and think of shriveled beetles crawling up a sticky milkweed. Creepy crawly yummy!

▶ *Difficulty: Easy*   ▶ *Serves 2*

4 stalks celery
4 teaspoons creamy peanut butter
4 teaspoons raisins

1. Cut the leafy part and the root part off of the celery. Wash the celery and dry it with a paper towel. Cut each celery stalk in half. Put 4 pieces on each plate.
2. Fill the indented ridge on each piece of celery with peanut butter.
3. Stick the raisins in the peanut butter.

*For some variety, you can substitute cream cheese or another soft cheese for the peanut butter and chocolate chips or dried cranberries for the raisins.*

# Oozing Pimples

The puss (cream cheese) will ooze into your mouth when you bite into these yummy pimples (cherry tomatoes).

▶ *Difficulty: Easy*   ▶ *Serves 1*

6 to 8 cherry tomatoes (or 2 small round tomatoes)
1 tablespoon soft cream cheese (plain or flavored)

1. Choose the biggest cherry tomatoes you can find. Rinse the tomatoes and pat them dry with a paper towel.
2. Use the end of a vegetable peeler (or a small paring knife) to core each tomato.
3. Stuff each tomato with the cream cheese. Put all the stuffed tomatoes on a plate.

# Lizard Eyes

Now you won't have to go to New Zealand to enjoy gecko eyes (crackers topped with cream cheese and kiwi), mate!

▶ *Difficulty: Easy*   ▶ *Serves 2*

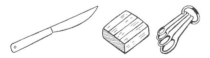

4 tablespoons cream cheese
8 round butter crackers (such as Ritz)
2 fresh kiwis

1. Spread a thin layer of cream cheese on each cracker.
2. Peel the kiwi and cut it into ½-inch slices.
3. Cover each cracker with a kiwi slice.

*Before taking a bite, give the pimple a gentle squeeze to "pop" it!*

**core** the center of a vegetable or fruit (such as an apple); to remove some of the inside of a fruit or vegetable, leaving the outer skin and enough flesh for the fruit to maintain its shape

Who likes gross things better: the daughter of a mortician or the son of a supermarket owner?

The son—he's a little grocer!

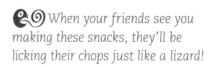

*When your friends see you making these snacks, they'll be licking their chops just like a lizard!*

## Frozen Walrus Tusks

These frozen, chocolate-covered bananas might look like walrus tusks, but they're absolutely dee-lish!

▸ *Difficulty: Medium*  ▸ *Serves 4*

4 ripe bananas
8 Popsicle or candy apple sticks
Waxed paper
3 ounces chocolate chips

1. Peel the bananas and cut each in half.
2. Shove a Popsicle stick or something that will work like a handle into the cut end of each banana half.
3. Cover a freezerproof plate with waxed paper.
4. Put 3 ounces (half a 6-ounce bag) of chocolate chips in a small, deep bowl. Melt the chocolate in the microwave, following the directions for your microwave.
5. Dip each banana into the melted chocolate, leaving it in and twirling it around enough to completely coat the fruit. Place the bananas on the plate.
6. Put the plate in the freezer for an hour or two. Remove from the freezer when you're ready for your snack.

*Frozen walrus tusks are a great snack for a summertime sleepover with your friends. For variety, you can roll these chocolate-covered bananas in something crunchy, like chopped nuts, Grape-Nuts cereal, crumbled Butterfinger candy bars, or toasted rice, before freezing them.*

What did the right eye say to the left eye?

Between us, something smells!

## PLAY IT SAFE:

Always use glass and other microwave-safe containers in microwave ovens. Never use plastic containers, which can melt, or metal containers, which can get too hot and cause sparks. If you're using a piece of pottery, such as a clay bowl, make sure that the bottom is stamped "made for microwave use." Some pottery and pottery glazes contain trace amounts of metals, which can be hazardous when heated in a microwave oven.

# Putrefied Eyeballs

You'll say "Yuk!" before and "Yum!" after you bite into a squishy eyeball (peeled grape with a blueberry pupil) floating in slime (Jell-O) and topped with flotsam (whipped cream).

▶ *Difficulty: Easy* ▶ *Serves 4*

2 cups water
1 (3-ounce) package Jell-O, any flavor (suggest Berry Blue or
   Strawberry-Kiwi)
20 large grapes
20 blueberries
4 tablespoons whipped cream (optional)

1. Boil 1 cup of water. While the water is boiling, dump the Jello-O powder into a plastic or heat-resistant glass bowl.
2. Pour the boiling water over the Jello-O powder. Stir until the granules are dissolved. Slowly stir in 1 cup of cold water. Put the bowl of Jell-O in the refrigerator to cool for 10 minutes.
3. While the Jell-O is cooling, wash the grapes and blueberries.
4. Peel the grapes. You should be able to do this with your fingers. With the end of a vegetable peeler, cut a small divot (about ¼ inch wide and deep) in one of the grapes. (Instead of using a vegetable peeler, you can use the tip of a paring knife to cut a small×in the grape.) Stick a blueberry into the slit. Repeat until all the eyeballs (grapes) have pupils (blueberries).
5. When the Jell-O is semi-firm (it jiggles a lot but doesn't splash when you shake it), remove it from the refrigerator. Plop the eyeballs into the gelatin. Return the bowl to the refrigerator until the Jell-O sets completely, about 2 to 3 hours.

### FREAKY FOOD FACT:
#### Hoof in Mouth?

One of the ingredients in gelatin is ground-up horse cartilage, which helps make the gelatin "gel." Cartilage is flexible bone tissue, like the stuff in your ears and nose. Horse hooves aren't made of cartilage. They're made of keratin, which is the same stuff your fingernails and toenails are made of.

*These slimy eyeballs look the most putrid floating in blue, pink, or green gelatin—and taste best when topped with a poof of whipped cream. To pucker you up, try Jell-O Ex-Treme Green Apple flavor.*

# Chicken-Fried Giant Grubs

Chewy guts will ooze over your teeth when you munch these baked grubs (breaded cheese sticks) dipped in warm blood (marinara).

▸ *Difficulty: Medium* ▸ *Serves 4*

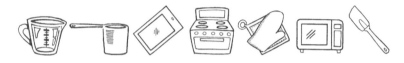

Cooking oil spray
1 egg
¼ cup milk
1 cup Italian-style breadcrumbs
8 sticks string cheese (or 1-ounce strips of mozzarella)
1 cup prepared spaghetti or pizza sauce, warmed in microwave

1. Spread a sheet of aluminum foil on a cookie sheet. Spray the foil lightly with vegetable oil (such as canola).
2. Break the egg into a large bowl and whisk for 30 seconds. Add the milk and whisk until the egg is broken up (but not frothy). Dip a cheese stick into the egg mixture and then into the breadcrumbs, coating completely. (You might need to dip it twice to thoroughly cover the cheese stick in egg and breadcrumbs.) Place the breaded cheese stick onto the cookie sheet. Repeat until all the cheese sticks are coated with crumbs and arranged on the sheet so they don't touch one another.
4. Let the cheese sticks set for 10 to 20 minutes. While the cheese sticks are setting, preheat oven to 400 degrees.
5. Bake in the oven 8 to 10 minutes, until the crumb coating is crunchy and the cheese is soft (the sticks will squish down with a spatula).
6. Remove the cheese sticks from the oven. Use a spatula to remove the cheese sticks from the cookie sheet and place them on a plate. Serve hot with warm marinara (pizza or spaghetti) sauce.

*For a tangy, tasty treat, dip your giant grubs in chilled phlegm (ranch dressing) rather than warmed blood (marinara).*

# Eewwww! Who Eats This Stuff?

Here's stomach-churning proof that one person's dream is another person's nightmare. Check out these freaky foods from around the world. On the line next to the food item, write the name of the place where you guess it is a disgustingly favorite munchie.

| | |
|---|---|
| Baked rooster combs _____ | United States (Southern) |
| Beef blood pudding _____ | Tibet |
| Bird's nest soup _____ | The Philippines |
| Blubber (raw whale fat) _____ | The Arctic |
| Boiled fish eyes_____ | Tanzania |
| Broiled beetle grubs _____ | Samoa |
| Deep-fried monkey toes _____ | Norway |
| Fried squirrel brain_____ | Nicaragua |
| Raw turtle eggs _____ | Mexico |
| Roasted bat _____ | Kenya |
| Salted, sun-dried grasshoppers _____ | Japan |
| Sautéed camel's feet _____ | Italy |
| Spoiled yak milk _____ | Indonesia |
| Warm cow urine _____ | France |
| White ant pie _____ | China |

## Hot Fresh Hippo Turd

This peanut-butter bread slathered with squished bananas smears all over your lips like globs of guts oozing over a chunk of hippo dung. Deliciously grotesque!

▶ *Difficulty: Hard* ▶ *Makes 1 loaf*

Cooking oil spray
2 cups flour
4 teaspoons baking powder
1 teaspoon salt

½ cup peanut butter
⅓ cup sugar (or honey)
1½ cup milk (or soymilk)
Fresh bananas

1. Preheat oven to 375 degrees.
2. Grease an 8×4×3-inch loaf pan with the cooking oil spray.
3. In a large bowl, combine the flour, baking powder, and salt.
4. In a separate bowl, mix together the peanut butter, sugar, and milk. Stir until mixed thoroughly and creamy. Add the peanut-butter mix to the flour mix. Stir well, until the wet and dry ingredients are all blended together and icky-sticky-gooey. Dump the batter into the pan, scraping the sides of the bowl to get all the goop. Spread the batter evenly in the pan.
6. Bake in the oven for 45 to 50 minutes, until the top of the bread is a crusty golden brown. Cool for about 10 minutes.
7. While the bread is cooling, peel a banana. In a small bowl smash the peeled banana with a fork or potato masher.
8. When the bread is cool enough to touch, slide the bread out of the pan and onto a cutting board. (Now it really looks like a big old hippo turd!)
9. Use a sharp, serrated knife to carefully slice off a chunk of bread (or ask an adult to do it for you). Spread the squished banana on the slab of hippo turd.

---

### FREAKY FOOD FACT:
### What Goes in Must Come Out

The average person eats three pounds of food a day. By the time you reach age seventy, that amounts to thirty-three tons of food—which comes out the other end to make a pile of poop the size of a car.

*Eat warm or at room temperature. To mix it up, slather with butter, margarine, or cream cheese and your favorite jam instead of bananas. Cover the leftover bread loaf snugly with plastic wrap to keep it fresh.*

# Funky Crunchy Skunk Bones

Toss some stinky (garlic and onion) croutons with grease (butter) and dried blood (paprika), toast them in the oven, and voila! Tasty bits of bones to die for!

▸ *Difficulty: Medium*  ▸ *Serves 4*

4 to 6 ounces garlic-and-onion croutons
½ cup (1 stick) butter
2 tablespoons sesame seeds
2 teaspoons celery salt
1 teaspoon paprika

1. Preheat oven to 275 degrees.
2. Pour the croutons into a large bowl.
3. In a smaller bowl, melt the butter in the microwave.
4. Combine the sesame seeds, salt, and paprika with the butter.
5. Pour the butter mixture over the croutons. Toss lightly with two wooden spoons until all the croutons are coated.
6. Spread the croutons out on a cookie sheet. Toast in the oven for 10 minutes, turn over the croutons and toast another 10 minutes. Cool before serving and eating.

🐌 *If you want to really gross out your family, breathe on them after eating a handful of these garlicky bits of skunk bones!*

**FREAKY FOOD FACT:**
**Puke Parlors**
Rumor has it that the royal palaces of ancient Romans had vomitoria, where people who had pigged out at a feast would go to vomit to make room for more food. After retching in the puke parlor, they'd return to the table and continue stuffing their faces. How revolting is that?

## Ghoul Fingers

It doesn't get much grosser or yummier than this: snacking on fermented fingernails (pepperoni) and cheesy corpse fingers (breadsticks)!

▶ *Difficulty: Medium*   ▶ *Makes 8 breadsticks*

1 (11-ounce) package refrigerated breadstick dough
8 slices pepperoni
Olive oil spray
Garlic salt, to taste
Grated Parmesan cheese, to taste
Marinara (prepared pizza or spaghetti sauce) or ranch dressing

1. Preheat oven to 350 degrees.
2. Separate the breadsticks and place on an ungreased cookie sheet.
3. Cut each slice of pepperoni into the shape of a fingernail.
4. Press a pepperoni fingernail onto the end of each breadstick. About ½ inch from the pepperoni fingernail, use a blunt knife to make 2 small knuckle creases. About 1 inch from the first knuckle creases, cut 2 more knuckle creases.
5. Spray the breadsticks lightly with olive oil.
6. Sprinkle the breadsticks with garlic salt.
7. Sprinkle the breadsticks with grated Parmesan cheese.
8. Bake according to the directions on the breadstick package (14 to 18 minutes).
9. Immediately remove the breadsticks from the cookie sheet and place on a plate.

🐛🌀 *Drizzle these ghoulish breadsticks with warm blood (marinara) or dip them in chilled bat saliva (ranch dressing).*

# Pigeon Poop

This sticky, icky cereal snack looks just like chunks of poop from a great big fat pigeon.

▶ **Difficulty:** *Medium*   ▶ *Makes 20 servings*

2 cups small pretzel sticks
5 cups Peanut Butter Crunch cereal (or any crunchy corn puff cereal)
3 cups Rice Krispies cereal (or any crisped rice cereal)
2 cups mini marshmallows
1 (12-ounce) bag white chocolate chips

1. Break the pretzels in half.
2. Mix the pretzel sticks, cereal, and marshmallows in a large bowl.
3. Dump the chocolate chips in a microwavable bowl and melt (about 1 minute).
4. Pour the melted chocolate over the cereal mix and toss lightly with a wooden spoon to make sure all the dry ingredients get wet.
5. Cover a large cookie sheet with wax paper. Spread the gooey mixture out on the wax paper to cool.
6. Once the gooey goop is set (cool and stuck together), break into chunks the size of a big splat of pigeon poop.

🐛🌀 *For a fun variation, substitute Cocoa Puffs cereal for the Peanut Butter Crunch.*

Why did the teacher say that Megan eats like a bird?

Because she snacks on worms!

## FREAKY FOOD FACT:
### True or False?
Sugar comes from grass.

*True! Sugar comes from sugar cane, which is a type of giant grass.*

# Funky Fridge

No wonder the cat barfed when Uncle Festus opened his funky old fridge! Find the one continuous line that runs from the top of the refrigerator (Start) to the bottom (End). Then color all of the sickening stuff that Uncle Festus should get out of his fridge!

# Chapter 5

# Digging Up Dinner

## Festering Burgers

Bet you can't wait to sink your teeth into this all-American favorite: burgers oozing with guts (cheese), crawling with worms (bean sprouts), and lathered in pus (mayo), blood (ketchup), and baby poop (mustard).

▶ *Difficulty: Medium*  ▶ *Makes 4 to 6 burgers*

1½ cups mung bean sprouts
1 cup cheddar cheese, shredded
1 pound ground beef (or ground turkey)
1 egg
Salt and pepper, to taste

4 to 6 hamburger buns (depending on the size of the burgers)
Mayonnaise (optional)
Ketchup (optional)
Mustard (optional)

1. Wash the sprouts with warm water and drain.
2. Shred the cheese (or just buy it already shredded).
3. Using your hands, mix 1 cup of the sprouts, the cheese, the ground beef, and the raw egg together in a large bowl.
4. Using your hands, form the burger meat into separate patties, all about the same size. (You'll be able to make 4 to 6 burgers, depending on how big you want each patty.) Place each patty on a cold griddle (or skillet).
5. Sprinkle salt and pepper on each burger.
6. Cook the burgers on the stovetop on medium heat until they are completely browned underneath. Carefully turn over the patties and cook on the other side until they are completely browned. When you press down on the burgers lightly with a spatula, no red juice should escape.
7. Place the burgers on open hamburger buns.
8. Sprinkle the rest of the bean sprouts (worms) on the hamburgers as a garnish. Serve with your favorite condiments: pus (mayonnaise), blood (ketchup), and baby poop (mustard).

*Instead of mung worms (bean sprouts), you can use stinky worms (onion cut in long strips). Serve on a plate with pickle slices and lettuce leaves that you've poked holes in so it looks like the worms have been munching on them.*

# Crunchy Pterodactyl Talons

These are ideal for dipping and crunching!

▶ *Difficulty: Medium* ▶ *Makes 4 servings*

Cooking oil spray
4 skinless, boneless chicken breasts
1 cup corn flakes
¼ cup warm water
¼ cup honey

8 to 10 large black olives, pitted
Your favorite dipping sauce
   (barbecue sauce, ketchup, honey,
   ranch dressing)

1. Preheat oven to 425 degrees. Spray the cookie sheet with oil.
2. Rinse the chicken in cold water and pat dry with a paper towel. Cut (or ask your adult kitchen helper to cut) the chicken into strips about ¾ inch wide.
3. Put the corn flakes in a clean paper lunch bag and roll the top of the bag twice to close it. (Instead, you can use a plastic food storage bag and seal it most of the way, leaving an opening for air to escape.) Roll the rolling pin over the bag until the corn flakes are crumbled. Put the crushed corn flakes on a plate.
4. Mix the warm water and honey together. If they don't mix, warm the honey water in the microwave on low for 15 seconds. One by one, dip the chicken strips in the honey water, and then coat with crumbled corn flakes. Place on a baking sheet, making sure there is an inch between each strip.
5. Bake in oven for 5 to 6 minutes, turn over the chicken strips, and bake for another 5 to 6 minutes, until the chicken strips are golden brown and cooked in the center. Remove immediately from the baking sheet and place on a serving platter.
6. Slice the olives in half lengthwise. You'll need 1 olive for every 2 chicken strips, so if you have 16 chicken strips, you'll need 8 olives. Place an olive half at one end of each chicken strip.

**CHEF'S SECRET:**
**Eggshells Be Gone!**
Crack eggs into a cup or a small bowl rather than into the mixing bowl. That way you can remove any bits of shell that fall into the egg when you crack it—before you mix the egg in with the other ingredients. Then you won't be crunching on egg shells when you chow down on your creations!

🐛🍳 *Serve these crunchy claws with blood (barbecue sauce or ketchup), bee spit (honey), or pureed pigeon poop (ranch dressing).*

## Fishtails and Ear Wax Fondue

You'll have an easier time making these juicy fish tails (tenders) with hot ear wax (cheese sauce) than you will scooping out the goop in your ears. These are tastier, too!

▸ *Difficulty: Easy*  ▸ *Makes 4 to 6 servings*

8 to 12 frozen fish sticks, fillets, or tenders
1 cup American cheese, shredded
Fresh lettuce
1 or 2 lemons

1. Arrange the frozen fish sticks on an ungreased cookie sheet or shallow baking pan.
2. Bake the fish in the oven according to the directions on the package (usually, at 400 degrees for 15 to 20 minutes).
3. Shred the cheese (or buy it already shredded). Put the cheese in a microwavable bowl. Melt the cheese in the microwave.
4. Wash and drain the lettuce. Separate into individual leaves, break off the root end, and pat dry with a paper towel. Place a lettuce leaf on each plate (or arrange them all on a platter).
5. Slice the lemon into wedges (or ask your adult helper to slice it). Place 2 or 3 fish sticks and a slice of lemon on each lettuce leaf.

🐌 *To add to the fun, serve these crunchy fish tails with three different dips: warm ear wax (cheese sauce), blood and guts (cocktail sauce), and boogers and snot (tartar sauce). Dip, bite, chew, and enjoy!*

### FREAKY FOOD FACT:
#### Eat with Feet
All humans have the ability to feed themselves with their feet. In fact, many people who have no hands or arms do just that. Of course, unlike butterflies—which eat and also taste through their feet—people ingest food through their mouths, and they taste food with their tongues and noses. (That's why you can't taste as well when your nose is stuffed up with boogers and snot.)

What do whales eat?

Fish and ships!

# Skewered Road Kill

Whether broiled in the oven or grilled over hot coals, these grilled teriyaki meat and vegetable shish kabobs are to die for!

▶ *Difficulty: Hard*  ▶ *Makes 8 servings*

1 (16-ounce) can pineapple chunks
⅓ cup soy sauce
1 teaspoon ground ginger
1 teaspoon brown sugar
½ teaspoon garlic salt
2 pounds top round steak (or skinned, boneless chicken breasts)

1 green bell pepper
1 zucchini, small to medium sized
Pearl onions
Cherry tomatoes

What do cats call mice on skateboards?

Meals on wheels!

1. Open the pineapple and drain the syrup into a large bowl.
2. To make the teriyaki marinade: combine the pineapple syrup with the soy sauce, ginger, brown sugar, and garlic salt.
3. Cut the steak (or chicken) into 1-inch cubes. Add the meat to the teriyaki marinade. Cover the dish with plastic wrap and let the meat stand at room temperature for 30 minutes. Turn the meat over to marinate the other side, pull the plastic wrap back over the dish, and let stand for another 30 minutes.
4. Wash the vegetables, drain, and pat dry with paper towels. Scoop the seeds out of the green bell pepper. Cut into 1-inch pieces. Cut the zucchini into 1-inch cubes.
5. When the meat has finished marinating, drain and discard the marinade. Assemble the shish kabobs, alternating the meat and vegetables on long skewer sticks. Broil the kabobs in the oven or on an outdoor grill, turning frequently until the meat is brown and the veggies are tender.

*Skewered teriyaki road kill is deliciously gross served with maggots (steamed or fried rice)!*

## Tapeworms and Hairballs

Your whole family will love sucking up these tapeworms (spaghetti) topped with hairballs (meatballs).

▶ *Difficulty: Hard*   ▶ *Makes 6 servings*

Olive oil spray
1 egg
½ medium onion, finely chopped
1 pound ground beef, lean
½ cup Italian breadcrumbs

½ cup grated Parmesan cheese
½ teaspoon salt
½ teaspoon ground black pepper
1 (1-pound) package spaghetti
3 to 4 cups prepared spaghetti sauce

1. Preheat oven to 350 degrees. Spray the bottom of a 9×13-inch glass baking dish with olive oil.
2. Break the egg into a bowl. Beat until the egg is yellow. Chop the onion into small pieces. Add to the bowl. Add the ground beef, breadcrumbs, Parmesan cheese, salt, and pepper to the bowl. Combine ingredients with your hands until well mixed.
4. Spray olive oil on the palms of your hands. Form the mixture into golf balls by rolling a fistful between the palms of your hands. Place the raw meatballs in the baking dish.
5. Bake the meatballs in the oven for 30 minutes.
6. Pour the spaghetti sauce into a large heavy saucepan. Use a big spoon to gently place the meatballs in the spaghetti sauce. Warm over medium-low heat, stirring occasionally.
7. Fill a large saucepan halfway with water. Add a dash of salt. Bring to a boil. Add the pasta to the boiling water, reduce the heat to medium high, and cook until tender, about 8 minutes.
8. Drain the pasta in a colander and rinse with cold water. Put the pasta on a serving platter or individual dinner plates. Use a ladle or large spoon to cover the tapeworms (pasta) with hairballs (meatballs) and blood (spaghetti sauce).

CHEF'S SECRET:
Milder Tomatoes
Tomatoes are an acidic food, but that doesn't mean your spaghetti sauce has to taste that way! Add a pinch of baking soda to your sauce to remedy this.

*Top each serving of tapeworms and hairballs with a tablespoon or two of dried pinworms (Parmesan cheese). If you want to spice and gross it up a notch, sprinkle some dried scabs (crushed red pepper) on top too!*

# Butchered Snake Bits

These chewy, juicy snake bits (sausage) are swimming in blood (barbecue sauce) and guts (grilled onion and green pepper)!

▸ *Difficulty: Medium*   ▸ *Makes 4 servings*

½ cup green bell pepper, diced
½ cup onion, diced
1 tablespoon vegetable oil
1 pound cooked mild sausage
1½ cups prepared barbecue sauce

1. Wash the green pepper and pat it dry with a paper towel. Clean out the seeds. Using a clean knife and cutting board, cut about half of the green pepper into very small pieces until you have ½ cup.
2. Peel the onion and dice it into very small pieces.
3. Heat the oil in a large saucepan over medium heat. Sauté the diced green pepper and onions until the onion is translucent, about 5 minutes.
4. Cut the sausage into bite-sized chunks. Put the meat in the saucepan.
5. Pour the barbecue sauce over the sausage, peppers, and onions in the saucepan. Cook over medium-low heat for about 30 minutes, stirring every 5 minutes.

🐛 *Serve heaped on a snake's nest (shredded lettuce or wilted spinach), open-faced over Texas toast, or in a sandwich roll.*

**PLAY IT SAFE:**
Never use the same knife and cutting board to cut two different foods. To prevent the spread of potentially harmful bacteria, always use a different knife and cutting board or wash the knife and cutting board with warm, soapy water before reusing it.

Why do maggots eat garbage?

It's a dirty job, but somebody's got to do it!

## Baked Hog's Head

The jelled blood (cranberry sauce) under the chinny-chin-chin of this severed pig's head (sliced ham with egg eyes, yam ears and nose, and pineapple smile) gives this gruesome entrée extra zing!

▸ *Difficulty: Medium*   ▸ *Makes 4 servings*

1 egg
1 sweet potato or yam
1 (1-inch thick) slice smoked ham (about 1 pound)
2 small black olives, pitted
1 (3-ounce) can pineapple rings
¼ cup jellied cranberry sauce

1. Boil an egg in a small saucepan filled halfway with water, about 8 minutes. Cool for about 10 minutes.
2. Preheat oven to 350 degrees.
3. Wash the sweet potato and pat dry with a paper towel. Cut three slices of sweet potato from the thickest part of the potato. Cut the tops off two of the slices so that one end of the slice is flat and the other end is rounded. These will be the pig's ears. Leave the third slice round (don't cut off the end) to use for the nose.
4. Place the ham slice in a shallow baking dish. Use a dish you can serve from. Position the two slices of sweet potato with the tops sliced off on the top rim of the ham slice, with the rounded side pointing downward, to make the hog's ears.

# Baked Hog's Head (continued)

5. Peel the egg. Cut a small slice off each end of the egg (to make the ends flat). Slice the egg in half. Position the egg slices about one-third of the way from the top rim of the ham slice and close together to make the pig's eyes.

6. Open and drain the olives. Slice 1 black olive in half lengthwise. Place the olive flat side down in the center of each egg slice to make the pupils in the pig's eyes. Place the round sweet potato slice directly under the eyes to make the pig's nose. Slice another black olive in half lengthwise. Position the olive slices flat side down on the nose to make the pig's nostrils.

7. Open the pineapple. Drain the juice into a small bowl and save. Slice 1 pineapple ring in half and position it directly under the pig's nose to form the pig's mouth. Place the rest of the pineapple rings in the baking dish, on either side of the hog's face. Mix the brown sugar with the reserved pineapple juice. Pour over the hog's head.

8. Bake in the oven for 30 to 35 minutes, until the sweet potato slices are tender.

9. Remove from the oven. Spread some jelled blood (cranberry sauce) under the pig's chin. Serve in the baking dish.

*Baked hog's head is superb served with a revolting side of Wormy Apples (page 82)!*

What do garbage collectors eat?

Junk food!

**FREAKY FOOD FACT:**
**Porking Out on Pork**
Americans eat 300 million sandwiches a year, and their favorite is a ham sandwich, followed by a BLT (bacon, lettuce, and tomato). Oink!

## Rotting Mummies

Bet you didn't know a rotting corpse (bean-and-cheese burrito) crawling with maggots (rice) could taste so good and be so disgustingly fun. Just watch your family's faces when they bite into the enshrouded head (tomato) and it pops and squirts into their mouths.

▶ *Difficulty: Medium*   ▶ *Makes 4 burritos*

1 cup cooked brown rice
4 small Roma tomatoes
½ cup red bell pepper, diced
½ cup onion, diced
1½ tablespoons vegetable oil
1 (15-ounce) can black beans
1½ teaspoons chili powder
1½ teaspoons garlic powder (or 2 garlic gloves, minced)
1 cup cheddar cheese, shredded
4 (12-inch) flour tortillas
2 cups chopped lettuce
¼ cup prepared salsa

1. Cook the rice according to the directions on the package. Let stand to cool.
2. Wash the tomatoes and red bell pepper and pat them dry with a paper towel. Remove the seeds from the pepper. Cut about half the pepper into small pieces.
3. Peel the onion. Cut about half the onion into small pieces.

What do you say to the kid next to you in the cafeteria who tries to take your cheese?

It's nacho cheese!

## Rotting Mummies (continued)

**4.** Heat the oil in a large skillet over medium heat. Cook the diced pepper and onion until you can see through the onion, about 3 minutes.

**5.** Pour the can of beans into a colander. Rinse and drain the beans. Add the beans to the skillet.

**6.** Stir in the chili powder and garlic powder. Cook the beans over medium heat for 3 minutes, stirring once about half-way through.

**7.** Add the rice and cheddar cheese to the skillet, and stir to mix together the ingredients. Cook over medium-low heat another 3 to 5 minutes, until the cheese melts, stirring once halfway through.

**8.** Warm the tortillas in the microwave for 5 seconds (or on a flat grill over low heat, about 15 seconds on each side). Spoon a strip of the rice-bean mixture onto the middle of each flour tortilla. The strip of filling should be about 3 inches wide and should go from the left edge of the tortilla to about 2 inches from the right edge of the tortilla. Place a tomato at one end of the rice-bean mixture to form the head of the mummy.

**9.** Wrap the burrito like this: (a) Fold the right flap of the tortilla over the filling; (b) Fold the bottom flap of the tortilla over the filling and tuck the edge under the filling; (c) Fold about 2 inches of the upper-right corner of the tortilla down sideways to make a small diagonal flap; (d) Fold the top flap of the tortilla over the filling.

*For older and grosser (and healthier) mummy shrouds, use whole-wheat tortillas.*

**FREAKY FOOD FACT:**
**French Froggie**
People in France (including kids) eat 200 million frogs each year.

# Turkey Eye Pie

These turkey eye pies (turkey meatballs in cheese pastry shells) take a little time to prepare, but they're totally creepy and tasty to gobble, gobble, gobble.

▶ *Difficulty: Hard*   ▶ *Makes 12 tarts*

¼ cup (half a stick) butter, softened
1½ tablespoons cream cheese, softened
1½ tablespoons milk
¾ cup flour
Dash salt
Cooking oil spray
1 egg, slightly beaten
¾ cup onion, diced
1 pound ground turkey
1¼ cup unseasoned bread crumbs
1½ teaspoon garlic powder
1½ teaspoons salt
1 teaspoon black pepper
⅓ cup processed cheese spread
¼ cup cheddar cheese, shredded
2 tablespoons vegetable oil
12 slices mozzarella cheese
6 large ripe black olives

### Step One: Make the Pastry Shell

1. In a large bowl, combine the butter and cream cheese until creamy.
2. Beat in the milk.

What did the cannibal order for take-out?

Pizza with everyone on it!

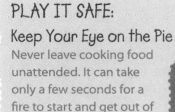

# Turkey Eye Pie (continued)

**3.** Add the flour and salt. Mix well and shape into a ball.

**4.** Cover and chill at least 2 hours.

**5.** Preheat oven to 425 degrees. Spray the cups of a miniature muffin tin with cooking oil.

**6.** Form about 1 tablespoon of dough into a small ball. Press the dough into a muffin cup, lining the bottom and sides with dough. Repeat until all the dough is used. Bake in the oven 4 to 6 minutes until the pastry is light golden brown. Cool.

*Step Two: Make the Meatballs*

**1.** Preheat oven to 350 degrees.

**2.** In a large bowl, beat the egg slightly.

**3.** Peel the onion. Cut into very small pieces.

**4.** Add the onion, ground turkey, bread crumbs, garlic powder, salt, and pepper. Using your hands, mix all the ingredients together well and form into 12 balls of about 2 inches each. Put the meatballs in a 9×13-inch baking dish. Bake in the oven for 30 minutes. Remove from the oven and cool.

*Step Three: Make the Turkey Eye Pies*

**1.** Preheat oven to 350 degrees.

**2.** Remove the pastry shells from the muffin pan and put them on a platter.

**3.** In a small bowl, combine the cheese spread and cheddar cheese.

**4.** Put a small blob of the cheese spread in each of the pastry shells.

**5.** Put a meatball on top of the cheese in each pastry shell.

**6.** Put a slice of mozzarella cheese on top of each meatball.

**7.** Cut the olives in half lengthwise. Place an olive half upside down (so the rounded part faces up) on each slice of mozzarella cheese. Bake in the oven 5 to 8 minutes, until the mozzarella cheese melts.

*For easier turkey eye pies, use prepared pastry shells and frozen meatballs from the grocery store. And if you want to make the eyes even grosser, place a few thin strips of pimento on each slice of mozzarella cheese.*

## Chopped Fooey

This concoction of chopped up critters and vittles (chicken and vegetables) takes a long time to stew. So make it on a rainy weekend when you have to play indoors anyway—or on a sunny day in an electric crock pot that doesn't need constant watching.

▶ *Difficulty: Medium*  ▶ *Makes 4 servings*

2 cups chicken broth
2 tablespoons soy sauce
1 tablespoon corn starch
1 teaspoon salt
1 teaspoon ginger (ground or minced crystallized)
2 whole chicken breasts (4 halves), skinned and boned
2 stalks celery, sliced
1 onion, sliced
1 (5-ounce) can water chestnuts, sliced
1 cup mushrooms, sliced
1 cup mung bean sprouts
¾ cup slivered almonds (optional)

1. In a crock pot (or a heavy soup pot), combine the broth, soy sauce, corn starch, salt, and ginger.
2. Cut the chicken into strips, about 2 inches long and ½ inch thick. Add to the pot. Wash the celery and pat dry with paper towels. Slice and add to the pot. Peel the onion. Slice and add to the pot.
3. Add the water chestnuts to the pot. Cover and cook on low for 5 to 6 hours. Then turn the heat to high.
4. Wash the mushrooms and pat dry. Slice the mushrooms and add to the pot. Add the bean sprouts to the pot. Cover and cook on high for 15 minutes.

**WORDS to KNOW**

**wok** a wide and deep pan with a rounded bottom used to stir-fry food in a small amount of very hot oil

*Serve soupy fooey on a heap of steamed maggots (white or brown rice) with broken bird bones (slivered almonds) sprinkled on top.*

# Slurp-ghetti

Calvin loves to go to the buffet on Tuesday nights! To find out why, color in the sections of his platter of pasta that have fleas (dots) on them.

## Blubber Roll-Ups

These are foul-looking (but good-tasting) fish roll-ups!

▶ *Difficulty: Medium*  ▶ *Makes 4 servings*

¾ cup cooked white rice
⅓ cup onion, minced
1 tablespoon vegetable oil
1½ cups fresh spinach, chopped
¾ cup mozzarella cheese, shredded
¼ cup Parmesan cheese, grated
1 egg white

1 teaspoon garlic powder
¼ teaspoon salt
⅛ teaspoon pepper
4 thin, flat fillets of white fish (sole or tilapia)
1 tablespoon lemon juice
Toothpicks

What fish smells like feet?

Fillet of sole!

Serve with lemon slices and shark's blood (cocktail sauce) or squid guts (tartar sauce).

1. Cook rice according to directions on the package. Set aside.
2. Peel the onion. Chop the onion into very small pieces. Heat 1 tablespoon of oil in a small skillet. Sauté the onion for about 5 minutes, until tender.
3. Wash and drain the spinach. Pat dry with paper towels. Remove the stems and tear the leaves into pieces.
4. Shred the mozzarella cheese. In a large bowl, combine the rice, onion, spinach, mozzarella cheese, Parmesan cheese, egg, garlic powder, salt, and pepper. Mix together well.
5. Cut each fish fillet lengthwise into two skinnier strips of about the same size, 2 to 4 inches wide (or have your adult kitchen helper do it for you).
6. Pour the lemon juice into a shallow glass 10-inch baking dish. Spread about ¼ cup of the rice mixture onto a fish fillet. Roll the fillet to enclose the filling. Skewer the roll-up with a toothpick to hold it together. Place the roll-up in the baking dish. Repeat for each of the fish fillets.
7. Microwave on high for 10 to 12 minutes, until the fish flakes easily with a fork. Let stand 5 minutes before serving.

# Dragon Bile

Tell your family that this stew (chicken and dumplings) came hurling out of the mouth of a fire-breathing lizard.

▶ *Difficulty: Medium* ▶ *Makes 6 to 8 servings*

1 pound chicken thighs, skinned and boned
1½ pounds chicken breasts, skinned and boned
2 celery ribs, sliced
8 cups chicken broth
2 tablespoons butter

1½ tablespoons flour
½ cup milk
Bisquick
Milk (for Bisquick dumplings)
1 (16-ounce) package frozen mixed vegetables

1. Cut the chicken into cubes (1-inch thick by 2-inches square).
2. Wash and drain the celery. Cut off the ends and throw away. Cut into thick slices.
3. Pour the chicken broth into a large, heavy-bottomed pot (such as a Dutch oven). Bring the broth to a boil over medium-high heat. While waiting for the broth to boil, melt the butter in a bowl. Add the flour to the melted butter, stirring to make a paste. Slowly stir in the milk. Add the milk mixture to the boiling broth, stirring constantly.
5. Reduce the heat to medium low. Add the chicken and celery. Cover the pot and cook 20 minutes.
6. While the chicken is cooking, prepare the dough for the Bisquick dumplings, following the directions on the box.
7. Return the stew to a boil over medium-high heat. Stir in the frozen mixed vegetables. Drop spoonfuls of the dumpling dough into the bubbling stew. Reduce heat to medium and cook uncovered for 10 minutes. Reduce heat to medium low, cover, and cook another 10 minutes.

**PLAY IT SAFE:**

When removing a lid from a cooking pot, always use an oven mitt and stand tall—never bend forward or put your face over the pot! Steam escaping from the pot can burn your skin and eyes.

*You'll know your dumplings are cooked to perfection when slimy on the outside (like they're covered in dragon saliva) and airy on the inside (like a biscuit).*

# Fish Eggs and Guts

There's nothing like a helping of fish gut (tuna noodle) casserole speckled with fish eggs (baby peas) and topped with a crunchy layer of crud (cheese-and-cracker topping) to make your family say, "It's so repulsive, it's delicious!"

▶ *Difficulty: Medium*  ▶ *Makes 4 servings*

2 cups elbow macaroni, cooked (about 4 ounces uncooked)
½ cup milk
1 (10-ounce) can cream of mushroom soup
¼ teaspoon garlic powder (optional)
1 teaspoon salt
⅛ teaspoon pepper
1 (7-ounce) package cooked tuna chunks, drained
1 cup frozen peas
¾ cup buttery crackers, crushed (such as Ritz)
½ cup grated Parmesan cheese

1. Fill a large saucepan about half full with water. Add a dash of salt. Boil the water over medium-high heat.
2. Cook the macaroni in the boiling water for 8 to 10 minutes, until the noodles are tender. Drain and rinse in a colander.
3. Preheat oven to 375 degrees.
4. Pour the milk into a casserole dish (1½ to 2 quarts).
5. Open the can of soup. Add the soup, garlic powder, salt, and pepper to the milk Use a fork to mix together well.
6. Open the can of tuna and drain all the liquid. Add the tuna, peas, and noodles to the casserole. Stir with a spoon.
7. Use a rolling pin to crush the crackers. Sprinkle the crushed crackers over the casserole.
8. Sprinkle the Parmesan cheese over the crushed crackers.
9. Bake in the oven for 10 minutes, until the casserole is heated all the way through and the topping is crispy.

## WORDS to KNOW

**al dente** an Italian word that means "to the tooth;" cooking pasta until it is tender but still firm and gives a slight resistance when you bite into it

*For the casserole topping, you can use dried scabs (corn flakes) instead of crackers and gassy cheese (Swiss cheese) instead of Parmesan cheese.*

# Ralpharoni Alfredo

Now you can produce a pile of puke (macaroni Alfredo) that tastes disgustingly good!

▶ *Difficulty: Easy*  ▶ *Serves 6*

2 cups mini macaroni, cooked (about ½ package of either ditali or tubetti pasta)
½ cup red bell pepper, diced
1½ tablespoons olive oil
1 cup fresh spinach, chopped (or frozen, thawed and drained)
1 cup small white beans (about half of a 15-ounce can)
½ teaspoon salt
⅛ teaspoon pepper
1 (26-ounce) jar prepared Alfredo sauce (2 to 2½ cups)
Romano cheese, grated (optional)

**FREAKY FOOD FACT:**
Which president introduced macaroni to the United States?
**A.** George Washington
**B.** Thomas Jefferson
**C.** Abraham Lincoln

*B. Thomas Jefferson, after visiting Italy.*

1. Fill a large saucepan half full with water. Add a dash of salt. Bring to a boil over medium-high heat.
2. Boil the macaroni in the water 8 to 10 minutes, until tender.
3. Drain the macaroni and rinse with cool water.
4. Wash the pepper and pat dry with paper towels. Remove the seeds and cut the pepper into small pieces.
5. Heat the olive oil in a skillet over medium-low heat. Sauté the pepper for 3 to 5 minutes, until tender.
6. Wash and drain the spinach. Remove the stems and throw away. Tear the spinach into smaller pieces.
7. Put the beans, macaroni, peppers, spinach, salt, and pepper in a glass (2- to 2½-quart) casserole dish and stir together. Pour the Alfredo sauce over the top and stir again, coating the pasta and beans. Microwave on high power for 4 minutes. Stir and microwave on high power for another 4 minutes or until heated all the way through.

*Top with a handful of grated Romano cheese. Leftover Ralpharoni makes a great lunch, too. Just store in a sealed container in the refrigerator, and then zap in the microwave tomorrow or the next day.*

# Find and Sing

Sing the "Diarrhea Song" on this page. If you don't know the melody, just make one up. Then, find the song's underlined words in the hidden-word puzzle and circle them. The hidden words go this way → and this way ↓.

## The Diarrhea Song

When you wake up in the morning,
Put your <u>feet</u> on the floor,
Do the 50-yard dash to the <u>bathroom</u> door,
Diarrhea, diarrhea!

When you're <u>sliding</u> into first,
And you feel something <u>burst</u>,
Diarrhea, diarrhea!

When you're sliding into third,
And you lay a <u>juicy</u> <u>turd</u>,
Diarrhea, diarrhea!

When you're sliding into home,
And you feel something <u>foam</u>,
Diarrhea, <u>diarrhea</u>!

| | | | | | | | |
|---|---|---|---|---|---|---|---|
| C | P | D | B | U | R | S | T |
| S | M | X | A | H | W | O | R |
| L | J | E | T | U | R | D | F |
| I | U | N | H | S | A | F | O |
| D | I | A | R | R | H | E | A |
| I | C | K | O | T | H | E | M |
| N | Y | B | O | J | E | T | O |
| G | R | E | M | L | D | V | G |

EVERYBODY SING!

# Chapter 6

# Sick Salads and Sides

Why doesn't the corn like the farmer?

Because he picks their ears!

## FREAKY FOOD FACT:
### True or False?
After you eat asparagus, your pee smells weird.

*True and false! Four out of ten people have a digestive enzyme in their stomachs that breaks down an acid found in asparagus. The digested asparagus acid makes their urine smell like sulfur.*

*If broccoli makes you want to barf, you can use an 8-ounce package of frozen corn and ¼ cup of blood clots (pimento) instead of the Birds Eye Broccoli, Corn & Peppers.*

# Puke au Gratin

Oh yeah! Scalloped corn definitely looks like vomit. It even feels like a mouthful of barf. Good thing it tastes extra good.

▸ **Difficulty:** *Medium* ▸ *Serves 6*

Cooking oil spray
1½ tablespoons butter (or margarine), melted
1 egg, slightly beaten
¾ cup milk
½ teaspoon salt
¼ teaspoon paprika
1 cup (half of a 1-pound bag) of frozen Birds Eye Broccoli, Corn & Peppers
1 (15-ounce) can creamed corn
⅓ cup cheddar cheese, grated
1 cup cracker crumbs (such as Ritz crackers)

1. Preheat oven to 350 degrees. Spray the inside of a large casserole dish with cooking oil.
2. Melt the butter in a microwaveable bowl or cup.
3. Beat the egg slightly, until it is partially blended.
4. Combine the butter, egg, milk, salt, and paprika in the casserole dish. Add the frozen mixed vegetables and creamed corn to the casserole and stir.
5. Sprinkle the grated cheddar cheese on top of the casserole.
6. Use a rolling pin to crush the crackers into fine crumbs. Spread over the casserole.
7. Bake in the oven for 45 to 50 minutes.

# Lemony Lice

Just try not to think about squirming lice and chewy head scabs when you eat this lemony couscous with dried cranberries!

▶ Difficulty: *Medium*  ▶ Serves 4

1 teaspoon lemon zest
1 tablespoon lemon juice (from 1 lemon)
2 cups chicken broth
½ teaspoon salt
⅛ teaspoon curry
1 tablespoon butter or margarine (or olive oil)
1 cup instant couscous
⅓ cup dried cranberries

1. Before cutting the lemon, grate the zest (lemon peel). Grate only the yellow part. The pieces of zest need to be very small, so your adult kitchen helper might need to cut the grated pieces into smaller pieces with a knife.
2. Cut the lemon in half. Squeeze the juice into a small bowl or cup. Remove the seeds.
3. Combine the lemon zest, lemon juice, chicken broth, salt, curry, and butter in a medium saucepan (1½ to 2 quart). Bring to a boil over medium-high heat.
4. Turn off the heat. Remove the pot from the burner. Stir in the couscous.
5. Cover and let stand for 10 minutes, until broth is absorbed. (Don't lift the lid during the 10-minute wait.)
6. Add the cranberries. Fluff up the couscous with a fork.

**CHEF'S SECRET:**
*Juicy Fruit*
Heavier lemons produce more, and tastier, juice. To get the most juice from a lemon, keep it at room temperature (don't refrigerate) and before squeezing it, roll it on a hard surface while pressing down with the palm of your hand. Or microwave it on low for about 30 seconds.

🐛👁 *Instead of scabs (cranberries), you can use ⅓ cup of boogers (cooked baby peas) or rabbit poop (raisins). By the way, couscous can be eaten warm or cold, so it makes a good side dish for dinner, school lunches, and picnics.*

## Sea Scum Drizzled in Eel Spit

Have you ever noticed the white scum left on the beach after a wave washes onto shore? Well, serve it as these smashed potatoes with a crater of eel spit (melted butter tinged a revolting brownish green)!

▶ *Difficulty: Medium*   ▶ *Makes 4 servings*

5 or 6 large potatoes (1½ to 2 pounds, Russet or baking potatoes)
⅓ cup milk
½ teaspoon salt

¼ teaspoon pepper
2½ tablespoons butter or margarine, melted
Red and green food coloring

1. Wash the potatoes. Peel off the skin with the vegetable peeler. Cut each potato into 1-inch cubes. Put the potato chunks in the colander and rinse with cold water.
2. Put the potato chunks in a large saucepan. Fill the pan with just enough water to cover the potatoes.
3. Cook the potatoes on high heat until the water boils. If it looks like the water might spill over the sides, reduce the heat. When the water starts to boil, reduce the heat to medium low. Cover the pot with a lid and cook 20 minutes, until the potatoes are tender when you poke them with a fork. Drain the potatoes and transfer them to a glass bowl.
4. Beat the potatoes with an electric mixer (or a potato masher) just until the potatoes are smooth. Stir in the milk, salt, and pepper while the potatoes are still hot.
5. Melt the butter in the microwave. Stir a drop of red food coloring and a drop of green food coloring into the melted butter. Use a big spoon to make a crater in the top of the smashed potatoes. Pour half of the melted butter into the crater and drizzle the other half over the top of the smashed potatoes.

*For added grossness (and flavor), sprinkle a few shakes of red mites (paprika) on top of the soap scum. If you like garlic, add ½ teaspoon of garlic powder when you stir in the milk, salt, and pepper.*

# Gangrenous Intestines

This slimy green pasta (buttered spinach linguine) is tossed with curdled crud (Parmesan cheese) for a savory side dish that's great with broiled fish or baked chicken.

▶ *Difficulty: Easy* ▶ *Makes 4 servings*

½ teaspoon plus a dash salt
½ pound spinach linguine or spaghetti noodles
2 tablespoons butter or margarine
½ teaspoon garlic powder
⅛ teaspoon ground pepper (black or white)
⅛ teaspoon basil (dried or fresh)
2 tablespoons Parmesan cheese, grated

1. Fill a large saucepan about halfway with cool water. Add a dash of salt.
2. Bring the water to a boil over high heat.
3. Reduce the heat to medium. Stir in the spinach noodles. Cook for 8 to 10 minutes, until the spinach noodles are tender but not mushy.
4. Drain the noodles in a colander. Rinse with cool water.
5. Return the noodles to the pan. Stir in the butter, salt, garlic powder, pepper, and basil.
6. Turn the burner to low. Stir in the Parmesan cheese. Toss the pasta with a large fork until the cheese is evenly distributed and starts to melt, about 2 minutes.

*For a healthier form of fat, substitute the butter with pigeon saliva (olive oil).*

What pasta has lots of pimples?

Zit-i!

**FREAKY FOOD FACT:**
Sniff and Taste
An apple, a potato, and an onion all taste sweet if you eat them with your nose plugged. Give it a try and see for yourself!

# Wormy Apples

These baked apples are rotten to the core (stuffed with apple butter) and squirming with worms (of the gummy variety).

▶ *Difficulty: Easy*  ▶ *Makes 4 servings*

Cooking oil spry
4 large apples
4 tablespoons apple butter
9 gummy worms

1. Preheat oven to 350 degrees. Spray the bottom of a baking pan with cooking oil (or grease with butter or margarine).
2. Core each apple from the stem end, leaving about ½ inch on the bottom. Do not push through the blossom end of the apple.
3. Spoon 1 tablespoon of apple butter into the hole of each apple.
4. Place the apples in the baking pan. Bake in the oven for 35 to 45 minutes, depending on the size of the apples, until the fruit is tender and the apple butter is bubbly.
5. Put each apple in a bowl. Spoon the syrup in the bottom of the baking pan on top of each apple. Slide 2 gummy worms into the hole of each apple so that half of the gummy worm is in the apple butter and half is sticking out of the apple.

🐌 *For spicier apples, put a stick of cinnamon in the squishy rot (apple butter) before baking.*

Say this tongue twister as fast as you can as many times as you can:

Frank fried fritters for fruit flies.
Frank fried fritters for fruit flies.
Frank fried fritters for fruit flies.

# Monkey Vomit

This is what happens when a monkey stuffs his belly with tropical fruit and coconut milk and then swings upside down from the branches (look out below!). Lucky for you, primate puke never tasted so good!

▶ *Difficulty: Easy* ▶ *Makes 4 servings*

1 (20-ounce) can pineapple chunks, drained
1 (11-ounce) can mandarin orange sections, drained
2 bananas, sliced
¼ cup shredded coconut
1 single-serving (6-ounce) container vanilla-flavored yogurt

1. Open and drain the pineapple and the oranges. Dump into the bowl.
2. Peel the bananas. Cut the bananas crosswise into slices. Put in the bowl with the other fruit.
3. Add the coconut and yogurt. Stir to mix together well.

🐚🌀 *It is best to eat monkey vomit (otherwise known as "ambrosia salad") immediately or store in the refrigerator for no more than a few hours before serving it. Otherwise, the pineapple will start to turn the yogurt into a watery mess, and the banana slices will start to turn brown.*

**CHEF'S SECRET:**
Banana Toots
Don't store bananas in a bowl or basket with other fruit. Bananas give off a gas that makes other fruit ripen and rot more quickly. And you thought people farts were silent but deadly!

**FREAKY FOOD FACT:**
A group of bananas is called:
**A.** A hand
**B.** A bunch
**C.** A cluster

*A. Each hand (group) of bananas has ten to twenty "fingers" (bananas).*

## Medusa's Dreadlocks

Dip these oven-fried dreadlocks (zucchini, carrot, and onion strips) into a bowl of snake spit.

▶ *Difficulty: Hard* ▶ *Serves 4*

Cooking oil spray
1 medium zucchini
1 medium carrot
½ medium onion
4 tablespoons Italian bread crumbs
1½ tablespoons Parmesan cheese
¼ teaspoon salt
⅛ teaspoon garlic powder
⅛ teaspoon paprika
⅛ teaspoon ground black pepper
3 teaspoons vegetable oil
1 tablespoon water
¾ cup ranch dressing
Green food coloring
1 medium black olive
1 baby dill pickle
1 red bell pepper strip

What did the skeleton say before eating?

Bone appétit!

1. Preheat oven to 475 degrees. Spray oil on a cookie sheet.
2. Rinse and drain the zucchini and carrot. Cut the zucchini in half lengthwise. Cut each of the 2 pieces in half lengthwise. Cut each of the 4 pieces in half crosswise. Cut the carrot in half crosswise. Cut each half into 4 carrot sticks.

## Medusa's Dreadlocks (continued)

3. Peel the onion and cut into thick slices. From the biggest slices, separate 8 to 12 of the outer rings. Cut 1 side of each ring so that it is no longer a ring and has 2 ends.

4. In a large zip-top plastic bag, combine the bread crumbs, Parmesan, salt, garlic powder, paprika, and pepper. Zip the bag to close it. Shake to mix together the ingredients.

5. Place the zucchini, carrot, and onion pieces in a different zip-top bag. Add the oil and water to the bag. Zip the bag to close it. Shake to wet the vegetables.

6. Place 2 or 3 of the wet vegetable pieces into the bread crumb bag. Close the bag and shake to coat the vegetables. Remove the veggies from the bag and place on a baking sheet. Repeat until you've breaded all the vegetables. Bake in the oven for 10 minutes, until golden brown and tender.

7. While the veggies are oven frying, pour the ranch dressing into a shallow bowl. Stir in a drop of green food coloring.

8. Slice the olive in half lengthwise. Carefully place each slice on top of the bowl of ranch dressing (Medusa's face), with the cut side down and the rounded side up, to form two eyes. Cut a slice of dill pickle on a diagonal. Use the tip of a sharp knife to make 2 small holes (nostrils) on the wider bottom of the pickle slice. (The easiest way to make a nostril is to stick the tip of the knife into the pickle and twirl the handle of the knife a few times.) Place the pickle slice on the ranch dressing to form Medusa's nose. Cut a thin strip of red bell pepper, about ½ inch wide by 3 inches long. Place on the ranch dressing to form Medusa's mouth.

9. Place the bowl on a platter. When the veggies are done baking, remove from baking sheet and arrange to form a semicircle of dreadlocks on the top edge of the bowl (Medusa's face).

In which country do people's tummies rumble most?

Hungary!

🐌🐚 *For creepier-looking Medusa locks, use this recipe to whip up a batch of oven-fried calamari (about ½ pound small squid, cut into thin strips), rather than veggies. Then dip it in squid guts (tartar sauce) rather than snake spit (ranch dressing).*

## Caterpillars and Chiggers

Chiggers are tiny red bugs that crawl all over your body and nibble on your skin, which then itches like the dickens. These giant shriveled chiggers (cranberries) combined with slimy green caterpillars (honey-coated green beans) will really make your skin crawl . . . and your mouth water.

▶ *Difficulty: Medium*   ▶ *Makes 4 servings*

2 cups fresh green beans
1 tablespoon orange juice
2 tablespoons honey
½ cup dried cranberries
¼ cup slivered almonds

1. Wash the green beans. Cut off the stems. Cut the green beans crosswise into bite-sized (2- to 3-inch) pieces.
2. Put the green beans in a large saucepan. Fill with water until it just covers the green beans.
3. Cook the green beans on the stovetop on medium-high heat for 8 to 10 minutes, until tender.
4. Drain the green beans using a colander. Return the green beans to the pot.
5. Stir in the orange juice, honey, cranberries, and almond slivers. Warm over medium heat, stirring constantly, for about 2 minutes.

### PLAY IT SAFE:

Never throw grease or water on a fire. The best ways to put out a small food fire is to smother it with a metal lid from a pot or to toss a few handfuls of baking soda over the fire. If a fire breaks out while you're cooking, get out of the way and let your adult helper take care of it.

*This recipe is easier to make using frozen cut green beans or canned green beans, but it tastes much better with fresh green beans, especially organic ones.*

# Bug-Eating Veggie Ogress

When this veggie ogress waddles through the garden, she sings a riddle: "I eat my dinner, and my dinner eats me." Get it? (The bugs eat her, and she eats the bugs.) Draw a line between the word and the object on the ogress.

Ant

Bee

Ladybug

Moth

Snail

Spider

Worm

Broccoli

Carrots

Corn

Eggplant

Peas

Pumpkin

Tomato

## Cow Cud

This is a great side for any gross-loving kid's meal!

▸ *Difficulty: Easy*   ▸ *Makes 4 servings*

½ cup alfalfa sprouts
1 medium carrot, grated
4 whole leaves of green lettuce

2 ripe avocados (Hass are best)
2 tablespoons Italian salad dressing

1. Wash and drain the alfalfa sprouts, carrot, and lettuce.
2. Grate the carrot.
3. Scoop the avocado into a bowl. Use a fork to mash the avocado until it is fairly smooth. Add the sprouts, carrots, and Italian dressing to the mashed avocado. Stir to mix well.
4. Use an ice-cream scoop to plop a mound of avocado salad onto each salad leaf.

## Diaper Dump

Get your baby doo-doo (chunky applesauce) while it's warm.

▸ *Difficulty: Easy*   ▸ *Makes 6 servings*

1 (24-ounce) jar prepared chunky
 applesauce (plain)
¼ cup raisins

1 teaspoon cinnamon
1 tablespoon brown sugar

1. In a large microwaveable bowl, combine the applesauce, raisins, cinnamon, and brown sugar. Stir together well.
2. Cover the bowl loosely with plastic wrap. Warm the applesauce in the microwave for 2 minutes. Stir and continue microwaving until warmed all the way through.

---

What animal pukes every time it eats?

A yak!

*For a healthy, tasty, disgusting-looking snack, spread cow cud on crackers or tortilla chips.*

**PLAY IT SAFE:**

When using a microwave, cover the dish with a lid or plastic wrap, but wrap it loosely so that steam can escape. The moist heat will help destroy potentially harmful bacteria, and the cover will keep the hot food from splattering all over the microwave and you.

*This chunky baby doo-doo is lip smackingly good cold, too.*

# Rotten Eggs

The best part about these spongy eggs (baby potatoes) is the putrid green slime (broccoli-cheese) covering them. It's enough to send shivers right up your spine.

▸ *Difficulty: Medium*  ▸ *Serves 4 to 6*

1 dozen small red potatoes
1½ cups broccoli florets
Pinch salt
8 ounces American cheese

1. Wash potatoes and broccoli.
2. Put the potatoes in a large saucepan. Add a pinch of salt. Fill with just enough water to cover the potatoes.
3. Put the broccoli in a separate saucepan. Fill with just enough water to cover the broccoli.
4. Cook the potatoes over medium-high heat for about 15 minutes, or until tender.
5. Cook the broccoli over medium-high heat for 8 minutes, or until tender.
6. Drain the potatoes. Put the potatoes in a serving bowl and cover to keep warm.
7. Drain the broccoli. Put the broccoli in the blender pitcher (or food processor).
8. Put the cheese in a bowl and melt in the microwave, following the directions for the microwave.
9. Pour the cheese in with the broccoli. Blend until the cheese turns green. Pour the green cheese over the potatoes.

**WORDS to KNOW**

**new potatoes** very small potatoes that are harvested early, before they can grow large; sometimes called "young" or "baby" potatoes, they have a thinner skin and their flesh is sweeter and firmer than mature potatoes

What is the difference between boogers and broccoli?

Kids don't eat broccoli!

🐌💿 *These foul-looking potatoes are great served with fowl (such as chicken, turkey, or Cornish hens).*

## Buzzard Innards

Repulse and delight your dinner guests with this steamy, creamy, blood-and-guts casserole made with spaghetti squash, chunky spaghetti sauce, and three different cheeses.

▸ *Difficulty: Hard*  ▸ *Serves 4 to 6*

1 large spaghetti squash
Cooking oil spray
2 cups mozzarella cheese, grated
1 cup Parmesan cheese, grated or
   shredded
1 cup cottage cheese

1 teaspoon salt
½ teaspoon ground black pepper
1 (26-ounce) jar prepared spaghetti
   sauce, chunky style with onion
   and bell pepper

1. Wash the squash. Cut it in half lengthwise. Clean out the seeds and pulp, leaving only the rind. *Note:* Spaghetti squash has a thick, tough rind, sort of like a pumpkin's, that is difficult to cut. So to be safe, your adult kitchen helper should cut the squash with a large, sharp knife or a cleaver.
2. Cook the squash in the microwave for 6 to 8 minutes. Let stand for at least 5 minutes.
3. Preheat oven to 350 degrees. Spray a large casserole dish with cooking oil.
4. Separate the strands of squash by running a fork lengthwise from stem to bottom and put them in the casserole dish.
5. Grate the mozzarella cheese (or buy it already grated).
6. In a bowl, mix together the mozzarella, Parmesan, and cottage cheeses and the salt and pepper.
7. Spoon half of the cheese mixture into the casserole dish. Mix it in with the squash. Stir in the spaghetti sauce.
8. Spread the other half of the cheese mixture on top of the casserole. Bake in the oven for 40 to 45 minutes.

**CHEF'S SECRET:**
**Make Your Own**
**Oil Sprayer**
Fill a clean spray bottle, which you can buy at most grocery and discount stores, with cooking oil from a bottle. When the oil runs out, just wash the bottle and refill it.

🐌 *Buzzard gut casserole goes great with a bowl of weeds (green salad) and garlic bread.*

# Spewed Salad

This gelatinous mess of chilled chunky vomit (pineapple-mandarin cole slaw in lime gelatin) topped with a dollop of bile (whipped cream and mayo topping) is sure to make everyone at the table gag with pleasure.

▶ *Difficulty: Medium*  ▶ *Serves 8 to 10*

What do you call a vegetarian with diarrhea?

A salad shooter!

1 (6-ounce) box green gelatin (lime or green apple)

2 cups cole slaw mix (shredded cabbage and carrots)

1 (8-ounce) can crushed pineapple, drained

1 (11-ounce) can mandarin orange segments, drained

2 cups whipped cream (or whipped cream substitute, such as Cool Whip)

½ cup mayonnaise

¼ teaspoon curry

1. Prepare the gelatin according to the directions on the box. Refrigerate 2½ hours, until partially set.
2. Wash and drain the cole slaw vegetables.
3. Open the cans of pineapple and mandarin orange, and drain off all the juice.
4. Put the cole slaw mix, pineapple, and mandarin orange in a large bowl or casserole dish. Use a fork to mix and mash it all together so that it looks like it's been chewed and digested. Pour the gelatin in with the veggie and fruit mixture, and gently fold it in with a wooden spoon.
5. Cover the gelatin salad with plastic wrap. Put in the refrigerator for 2 to 4 hours, until it has the consistency of a giant glob of fresh, shiny puke.
6. In a separate bowl, mix together the whipped cream, mayonnaise, and curry. Cover and refrigerate until you're ready to serve the gelatin.

🐛🐌 *Top each serving of spewed salad with a glob of dry-heave foam (the whipped-cream and mayo topping).*

# Poo-ey!

All of these foods have one thing in common: They're odiferous! Use the letters from the word S T I N K Y to complete these foul-smelling food words.

## S T I N K Y

v i n e g a r

Bru _ _ el _  _ prou _ _

blu _  chee _ e

_ u _ a  f _ _ _ h

mold _  bread

ro _ _ e _  egg _

_ po _ led  mil _

ra _ _ c _ d  mea _

Chapter 7

# Disgusting
# Desserts

## Troll's Toes

Dip these troll's toes (sugar cookies) in toe jam (apricot jam)!

▶ *Difficulty: Hard*  ▶ *Makes about 4 dozen cookies*

| | |
|---|---|
| 1 cup (2 sticks) butter or margarine, softened | 2¾ cups flour |
| 1 cup sugar | 1 teaspoon baking powder |
| 1 egg | 1 teaspoon salt |
| 1 teaspoon almond extract | Cooking oil spray |
| 1 teaspoon vanilla extract | 1 small tube green cake decorating gel |
| | ¾ cup whole blanched almonds |

1. In a large bowl, combine the butter, sugar, egg, and almond and vanilla extracts. Beat together until creamy.
2. In a separate bowl, combine the flour, baking powder, and salt.
3. Pour the dry mixture into the wet mixture. Beat until all of the dry ingredients are mixed in and the batter is smooth. Cover the dough and put it in the refrigerator for 30 minutes.
4. Preheat oven to 325 degrees. Spray cooking oil on a cookie sheet.
5. Divide the dough into 4 equal pieces. Leave one piece out and put the rest back in the refrigerator.
6. Place a heaping teaspoon of dough on a pastry board (or a sheet of waxed paper). With your hands, roll the dough and shape it into fat toes. Squeeze the edges together about one-third of the way down each toe to form a knuckle shape. Squeeze a small dab of decorating gel on the tip of each toe. Put an almond on the gel and press to secure the toenail. Use a blunt knife to make two knuckle lines across each toe.
7. Arrange the cookies on a cookie sheet. Bake for 20 to 25 minutes, until golden brown. Let cool 3 minutes. Remove from the cookie sheet and put on a wire rack to cool.
8. Repeat steps 6 through 9 until you've used up all the dough.

CHEF'S SECRET:
No-Spill Measuring
To measure small amounts of liquids—such as vanilla extract—use a medicine dropper with measurements marked on it. You can find these droppers in drugstores.

*These troll's toes spread while baking, so form the dough a little smaller than you want the toes to be.*

# Barf Biscuits

It's a good thing these no-bake peanut butter and oat-meal cookies are mouth-wateringly scrumptious, because they look like splats of dried puke.

▸ *Difficulty: Medium*   ▸ *Makes about 3 dozen cookies*

Waxed paper
2 cups sugar
½ cup milk
¼ cup semi-sweet or unsweetened cocoa powder
½ cup (1 stick) butter or margarine
1 teaspoon vanilla
½ cup peanut butter
3 cups quick-cooking oatmeal

**FREAKY FOOD FACT:**
Schlurrp!
Food can only be tasted if it's mixed with saliva. So if you see slobber running down someone's chin while they're eating, chances are the food is extra tasty!

1  Line the bottom of a large glass baking pan or plastic storage container with waxed paper.

2. Combine the sugar, milk, cocoa, and butter in a large saucepan.

3. Stir constantly over medium-high heat to blend ingredients and bring to a boil. Let boil for exactly 1 minute. Remove pan from heat.

4. While still warm, stir in the vanilla, peanut butter, and oatmeal.

5. Let cool for 5 minutes. Drop by teaspoons onto the waxed paper. With the back of the spoon, press down on the batter to squash it into a thick disk shape.

6. Refrigerate until the cookies are chilled and chewy (firm).

*To make these barf biscuits look even more revolting, add ½ cup of spewed nuts (chopped peanuts).*

## Grubs in Dirt

Chocolate pudding mixed with Oreo cookie crumbs and chopped up gummy worms looks and feels likes slimy, gritty mud crawling with repulsive bugs.

▶ *Difficulty: Easy*  ▶ *Serves 6*

1 small box chocolate pudding, instant or cooked
12 chocolate sandwich cookies (such as Oreos)
6 gummy worms (preferably yellow, white, or clear)
6 flat-bottomed ice-cream cones

1. Prepare the pudding according to the directions on the box. (Let cooked pudding cool to room temperature.) Spoon the pudding into a bowl.
2. Crush the Oreos into small crumbs.
3. Use a blunt knife to cut the gummy worms into 1-inch pieces.
4. Stir the gummy worm pieces and half the cookie crumbs into the pudding.
5. Spoon the pudding mixture into each of the ice-cream cones.
6. Sprinkle the rest of the cookie crumbs on top of the pudding in the cones.

👁 *Want to really disgust your parents? Take a bite of grubs in dirt, swish it around your mouth without swallowing, and then give your folks a big toothy smile.*

FREAKY FOOD FACT:
Pass the Moss, Please
A type of seaweed called carrageen moss is often used as a thickener in pudding and ice cream.

CHEF'S SECRET:
To Make Cookie Crumbs
Seal the cookies in a plastic zip bag. Use a rolling pin to crush the cookies.

# Puppy Chow

No gross cookbook for kids would be complete without this classic: Chex cereal coated with melted chocolate and peanut butter and dusted in powdered sugar.

▶ *Difficulty: Medium* ▶ *Makes 10 servings*

2 cups semi-sweet chocolate chips
½ cup (1 stick) butter or margarine
⅓ cup peanut butter
9 cups Corn or Rice Chex cereal
2 to 4 cups powdered sugar

1. Put the chocolate chips, butter, and peanut butter in a microwaveable bowl. Melt the ingredients together in the microwave, following the directions for the microwave. Stop the microwave about halfway through the melting time and stir the mixture at least once. Make sure everything is completely melted.
2. Stir the melted ingredients to blend together.
3. Pour the cereal into a very large bowl.
4. Slowly pour the chocolate mixture over the cereal. Gently fold (turn over) the cereal until it is all completely coated with the chocolate mixture.
5. Put the powdered sugar into a large, clean paper bag.
6. Dump the cereal into the bag. Shake until all the cereal is covered. Add more sugar if needed.

*This crunchy concoction could easily pass for puppy chow—minus the stench and taste of liver and lamb meat.*

**FREAKY FOOD FACT:**
**Smeared Science**
The microwave oven was invented by a scientist after he walked by a radar tube and a chocolate bar in his pocket melted.

# Spurting Spider Cake

When you slice into this black cake filled with lime Jell-O, the green "guts" spurt out all over the place. Yuck!

▸ *Difficulty: Hard* ▸ *Serves 4*

| | |
|---|---|
| 1 (3-ounce) box green Jell-O (lime) | Blue food coloring |
| 1 box yellow cake mix | 8 black licorice sticks |
| 1 can prepared chocolate frosting | 2 large red gumballs or gum drops |

1. Prepare the Jell-O according to the directions on the box. Put in the refrigerator and chill until the gelatin sets completely.
2. Prepare the cake batter according to the directions. Pour into two 9-inch round cake pans that have been greased and floured. Bake according to box instructions. Remove from the oven and let cool to room temperature. Spoon the frosting into a bowl. Stir in blue food coloring until the frosting turns black.
3. Remove the set Jell-O from the refrigerator. Use a spoon to churn it up so that it looks like green guts.
4. Remove the cakes from the pans. Put a few dabs of frosting on a baking sheet. Cut a 5-inch circle out of the center of the cake. Set the small circle aside for the spider's head.
5. Put a few dabs of frosting under the cake to hold it in place. Fill the hole in the cake with Jell-O. Put the uncut layer of cake on top of the filled layer. This is the spider's body.
6. Spread a 3-inch swab of frosting along the edge of the larger cake. Place the smaller cake against the frosting. Spread frosting over the entire cake. To make the legs: bend the licorice in a rainbow shape; stick one end near the top of the cake and then drape the stick downward. Put the gumball eyes on the spider's face.

What is brown, hairy, and wears sunglasses?

A coconut on summer vacation!

🌀 *To make a tarantula, use coconut-pecan frosting (the kind used for German chocolate cake) instead of chocolate frosting.*

# Bloody Bug Pops

These homemade popsicles are made with yogurt and berries, blended together in a mushy mess.

▶ *Difficulty: Medium*   ▶ *Makes 8 pops*

½ cup red berry juice (cranberry, raspberry, cherry—your choice)
1 envelope unflavored gelatin
1 cup vanilla yogurt
1 cup fresh or frozen blueberries
8 small (3-ounce) paper cups
Aluminum foil
8 Popsicle sticks or plastic spoons

1. Pour the berry juice into a saucepan. Add the gelatin.
2. Warm the juice mixture on the stove over low heat, stirring constantly until the gelatin dissolves completely.
3. Pour the juice mixture into a blender. Add the yogurt and blueberries. Blend for about 2 minutes.
4. Pour the blended juice into the paper cups.
5. Cover the top of each cup with foil. Poke a wooden stick (or the handle end of a plastic spoon) in the middle of each paper cup, about 2 inches deep or far enough so that it stays in place.
6. Put the cups on a cookie sheet (or plastic tray). Put in the freezer for about 3 hours, or until frozen all the way through.

*When it's time to eat or serve the pops, remove from the freezer and let stand at room temperature for about a minute. Then peel off the paper cup and the foil, and lick and slurp your frozen bloody bug juice.*

**FREAKY FOOD FACT:**
**The First Bugsicle**
The Popsicle was invented in 1905 by an eleven-year-old boy named Frank Epperson. He accidentally left a cup of soda pop outside with a stir stick in it. When he went to retrieve his drink hours later, it had frozen (no doubt with a bug or two in it). When he grew up, Frank Epperson patented his concoction and called it the "Epsicle." The name was later changed to "Popsicle."

## Giant Snails

Cinnamon rolls never tasted so great and looked so creepy crawly!

▶ Difficulty: *Medium*   ▶ *Makes 4 servings*

Cooking oil spray
¼ cup finely chopped walnuts or pecans (optional)
3 tablespoons sugar

½ teaspoon ground cinnamon
Waxed paper
1 package (8) refrigerated breadsticks
4 chocolate chips

1. Preheat the oven to 375 degrees. Spray the cookie sheet with cooking oil.
2. In a mixing bowl, stir together the nuts, sugar, and cinnamon. Pour into the pie pan and spread evenly over the bottom.
3. Lay a large sheet of waxed paper on the counter (or table).
4. Remove two rolled-up breadsticks from the package and put on the waxed paper. Unroll 1 of the breadsticks. Press one end of the unrolled breadstick onto the end of the rolled up breadstick. To make the snail's head, take the other end of the unrolled breadstick and roll the top of it under in the other direction.
5. Lift the snail carefully and put it in the pie pan. Gently flatten the snail with the palm of your hand.
6. Remove the snail from the pie pan and place it sugared side up on the cookie sheet. (If the head separates from the body, just press them back together after you put them on the sheet.) Place a chocolate chip eye on the head.
7. Repeat steps 4, 5, and 6 until you've made all four snails.
8. Bake for 15 minutes, or until the bread crust is golden.

Say this tongue twister as fast as you can as many times as you can:

Ben's bun is better buttered, he muttered.
Ben's bun is better buttered, he muttered.
Ben's bun is better buttered, he muttered.

🐌 *Serve warm or cool. Enjoy your giant sea snails warm and slithery, with melted butter on top.*

# Mud Pie

Here's the real deal: a mud pie you can actually eat (without worrying about getting pinworms) because it's made with wafers, ice cream, and nuts—rather than dirt, water, and gravel.

▶ *Difficulty: Easy*  ▶ *Makes 8 servings (1 pie)*

1 quart coffee or mocha ice cream, softened
1 premade packaged chocolate pastry crust (9-inch)
Aluminum foil
1½ cups chocolate fudge sauce
½ cup whipped cream
¼ cup chopped nuts (optional)

**FREAKY FOOD FACT:**
Hot 'n Cold!
People in Tokyo, Japan, eat horseradish ice cream.

1. Spoon the ice cream into the pastry crust and spread evenly with a rubber spatula.
2. Cover with foil and place in the freezer until the ice cream is firm, at least 1 hour.
3. Remove the ice-cream pie from the freezer. Spread fudge sauce over the top. Return to the freezer for 10 hours (or overnight).
4. Just before serving, top with whipped cream and chopped nuts.

*If you don't like gravel (chopped nuts) on your mud pie, you can sprinkle dirt (crushed chocolate wafers) on top instead.*

A boy was spending the day at his grandparent's house while his mom went shopping with his grandma. When his grandpa left the room to go to the bathroom, the boy gobbled down a bowl of peanuts that was sitting on the coffee table. Later that afternoon, as the boy and his grandpa played checkers together, the boy started to feel guilty. He told his grandpa how sorry he was for eating the peanuts without asking permission. "Oh, that's okay. I never eat the peanuts anyway," his grandpa said. "Since I lost my teeth, all I can do is suck the chocolate off the M&Ms."

Store leftover petrified rabbit turds in plastic bag or container that seals.

## Petrified Rabbit Poop

Bet you can't eat just one handful of these caramelized peanuts, which look and crunch just like petrified bunny turds!

▸ Difficulty: Medium ▸ Makes 4 servings

Aluminum foil
Cooking oil spray
1 egg white
1 teaspoon cold water
16 ounces shelled peanuts
1 cup brown sugar, packed
¼ teaspoon salt

1. Preheat the oven to 225 degrees. Line a cookie sheet with foil and spray with cooking oil.
2. Separate the egg white from the yolk. (You might need an adult's help to do this.) You won't need the yolk for this recipe.
3. In a large bowl, combine the egg white and water. Beat with mixer (or whisk) until frothy (not stiff).
4. Stir in the peanuts until they're completely coated with egg goo.
5. Spread the peanuts over the cookie sheet.
6. In a separate bowl, combine the brown sugar and salt. Pour over the peanuts.
7. Bake for 1 hour, stirring and turning over every 15 minutes.

# Armpit Hair

If they didn't smell and taste so yummy, eating these chewy clumps of chocolate-covered Shredded Wheat armpit hairs could make your stomach heave.

▶ *Difficulty: Medium*  ▶ *Serves 8 to 10*

3 large Shredded Wheat cereal bundles
3 tablespoons honey
1 tablespoon brown sugar
1 (6-ounce) bag chocolate chips
2 tablespoons butter or margarine
Waxed paper

1. In a rectangular baking pan (9×13-inch), unravel the Shredded Wheat into long strands, so they look like armpit hairs. Set aside.
2. In a medium-size microwaveable bowl, combine the honey, brown sugar, chocolate chips, and butter. Heat on low in the microwave, stirring every 1 to 2 minutes, until melted.
3. Pour the chocolate mixture over the Shredded Wheat. Use a rubber spatula to gently turn over the cereal until it is coated with the gooey chocolate mixture.
4. Line the bottom of a cookie sheet (or flat tray) with waxed paper. Spoon the chocolate-coated Shredded Wheat onto the waxed paper, making 8 to 10 clumps of equal sizes.
5. Use a fork to gently rake the wheat strands (hairs) in one direction.
6. Put the "hairy" candy in the refrigerator for 30 to 45 minutes before serving.

**FREAKY FOOD FACT:**
True or False?
Eating chocolate causes acne.

*False. That's just an old wives' tale. Contrary to popular belief, the sugar and small amount of caffeine in chocolate don't make you hyper, either. But if you eat too much, the high fat content of chocolate can give you diarrhea.*

*Make sure to store any leftover clumps of armpit hair in the refrigerator.*

## Moo Patties

These look like the poop piles found in a field of calves.

▶ *Difficulty: Hard*  ▶ *Makes about 2 dozen cookies*

| | |
|---|---|
| 1 (3-ounce) package lime Jell-O | 2 teaspoons vanilla |
| 1 cup hot water | 1¾ cup flour |
| 1 cup sweetened shredded coconut | 1 teaspoon baking soda |
| 1 cup (2 sticks) butter, softened | 1 teaspoon salt |
| ¼ cup sugar | 2½ cup quick-cooking oats |
| ⅔ cup brown sugar, packed |    (oatmeal) |
| 2 eggs | 1 cup chopped walnuts |
| 2 tablespoons milk | 1 cup raisins (or currants) |

1. Preheat oven to 375 degrees.
2. Mix Jell-O and hot water in a bowl. Stir until the gelatin is completely dissolved. Stir the coconut into the Jell-O. Set aside.
3. In a large bowl, combine the butter, sugar, and brown sugar. Beat until creamy. Add the eggs, milk, and vanilla to the sugar mixture. Beat until blended together. Set aside.
5. In a small bowl, combine the flour, baking soda, and salt.
6. Add the flour mixture to the wet mixture. Stir to combine. Stir the oats, nuts, and raisins into the cookie dough.
8. Pour the coconut into a colander and let the Jell-O drain from the coconut. Spread the coconut on two paper towels. Put two more paper towels on top. Press down with the palm of your hand to squeeze out the extra liquid.
9. Spoon rounded tablespoons of dough on an ungreased cookie sheet. The patties will spread during baking, so space them 1½ to 2 inches apart. Bake 9 minutes, until golden brown (the coconut will be green). Allow the patties to cool on the cookie sheet for 1 minute before moving them to a wire rack.

Two flies were sitting on a pile of poo. One fly passed gas. The other fly said, "Hey, do you mind? I'm eating here!"

*After chomping down one of these chewy cow patties, you'll want to bellow, "Moooo-ore!"*

# Tongue on a Stick

Here's a fun way to totally gross out your whole neighborhood: Walk down the street licking one of these meringue tongues on a stick!

▶ *Difficulty: Hard*  ▶ *Makes 12 servings*

6 egg whites
1 cup sugar
Red food coloring

Parchment paper
12 Popsicle sticks
Pink or red cake crystals

1. Put the oven rack on the lowest level. Preheat the oven to 200 degrees.
2. In a large bowl, separate the egg whites from the yolks. Make sure no yolk falls into the bowl. (You might need an adult's help to do this.) You won't need the yolks for this recipe. With an electric mixer, beat the egg whites rapidly until soft peaks start to form. Slowly stir in the sugar, one spoonful at a time. Continue to beat until the mixture forms stiff and shiny peaks. Gently stir 2 or 3 drops of red food coloring into the meringue.
3. Line the bottom of a cookie sheet with parchment paper.
4. Spoon about 3 tablespoons of meringue onto the parchment paper. Use the curved part of the spoon to shape the meringue into the shape and size of a tongue. Repeat until you've used up all the meringue.
5. Gently press a Popsicle stick into the center of each tongue, leaving about a 2-inch handle sticking out of the wider end of the tongue.
6. Sprinkle the cake crystals over the tongues. Bake for 2½ to 3 hours, until the tongues are completely dry to the touch. Allow to cool completely before carefully removing the tongues from the parchment paper with a spatula.

**CHEF'S SECRET:**
To Separate Egg Whites
Hold a raw egg in one hand, with the narrow end pointing up. With your other hand, use a fork to poke a small hole in the pointy end of the egg. Turn the egg upside down over a small bowl, and gently shake and twist the egg until the clear part (the egg white) all comes out of the hole and just until the yolk reaches the hole.

To create the grossest tongues you'll ever love to eat, use a pastry brush to spread a thin layer of "mucous" (marshmallow topping, melted in the microwave) on each baked and cooled tongue, and then sprinkle with "hair" (chocolate cake sprinkles).

# Eat Dirt!

Complete this color-by-letters puzzle to uncover a gritty, grubby, yummy dessert in this chapter.

Color each space with the letters in P-O-O-P brown.
Color each space with the letters in B-A-R-F blue.
Color each space with the letters in G-U-T-S red.
Color each space with the letters in M-I-L-D-E-W yellow.

# Chapter 8

# Burps
# and Slurps

## Slug Spit

On hot summer days when slugs hide in the shade, you can cool off by slurping on a frosty glass of slimy, tangy slug spit (banana-lime slush).

▶ *Difficulty: Easy*  ▶ *Serves 2*

13½ ounces limeade (or other green citrus fruit drink)
1 (¼-ounce) envelope unflavored gelatin
1 banana, sliced
Green food coloring
Yellow food coloring
6 large ice cubes

1. Pour ¼ cup limeade in small saucepan. Sprinkle the gelatin over the juice. Let stand 1 minute.
2. Stir the gelatin into the fruit drink. Heat over low heat, stirring constantly, until gelatin dissolves. Remove from heat.
3. Peel and slice the banana.
4. Put the banana slices and the rest of the fruit drink in a blender. Cover and mix until smooth.
5. Add the gelatin mix and the green and yellow food coloring. Cover and mix 1 minute.
6. Add the ice cubes to the blender, cover, and blend on high speed for 1 to 2 minutes until slushy.

*Pour the slug spit into glasses and serve immediately. Slurp slowly, so you don't get brain freeze!*

### PLAY IT SAFE:
Never stick a spoon, spatula, or any other utensil in a blender while it's running. Not only can it make a mess, with food splattering all over the place, but the utensil can break and then slivers of wood or metal could fly out and injure you.

### CHEF'S SECRET:
To Stop Brain Freeze
Press your tongue to the top of your mouth, which warms the palate.

# Bloody Hairy

The toasted coconut floating in this raspberry-lemonade spritzer feels like hair in your mouth. Disgusting!

▶ *Difficulty: Medium* ▶ *Serves 6*

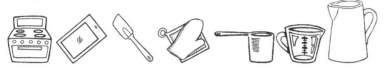

1 cup shredded coconut
3 cups raspberries (fresh or frozen)
6 ounces lemonade (fresh or from frozen concentrate)
1 quart ginger ale

1. Preheat oven to 350 degrees.
2. Spread the coconut on the bottom of an ungreased cookie sheet.
3. Toast the coconut in the oven 5 to 10 minutes, until golden brown. Stir and flip over the coconut two times while it's toasting. Remove from pan and let cool.
4. Rinse and drain the raspberries. Put them in a bowl and mash them with a fork.
5. Put the smashed raspberries, lemonade, and ginger ale in a large pitcher. Stir to mix.
6. Put a handful of toasted coconut in the bottom of each glass.
7. Slowly pour the berry spritzer over the coconut.

What do you call a cat that has eaten a lemon?

A sour puss!

🐛🍬 *When you pour the bloody pulp (bubbly raspberry lemonade) into a glass, the hair (toasted coconut) will rise to the top with the foam.*

## Septic Soda

This chocolate frappe with bits of dried poop (chocolate chips) floating in it is grotesquely good to the last gulp!

▶ *Difficulty: Easy*   ▶ *Serves 4*

1 quart chocolate chip ice cream, softened
¾ cup chocolate syrup
1 liter (1 quart) club soda
4 small Tootsie Rolls (optional)

1. Let the ice cream sit on the counter at room temperature for a few minutes, until it is soft enough to scoop easily.
2. Fill tall glasses about half full with ice cream.
3. Pour 3 tablespoons of chocolate syrup in each glass.
4. Slowly pour the soda into each glass and fill almost to the top, leaving about 1 inch from the rim.
5. Stir well with a spoon.
6. Serve immediately with spoons (iced-tea spoons are best) so you and your guests can scoop out all the chunks of "poop" (chocolate chips).

🐛🌀 *You can use vanilla, chocolate, or mint chocolate chip ice cream for your septic soda. We especially like the revolting mildew-green color of the mint flavor. Septic soda is even more disgusting with a turd (unwrapped mini Tootsie Roll) pressed onto the rim of each glass.*

**FREAKY FOOD FACT:**
Good Belching!
The Excuse Me company in Colorado makes a super-fizzy red soda pop called Rudy Begonia's Belcher.

**CHEF'S SECRET:**
Got Milk Skitters?
For people who are lactose intolerant—meaning they often get diarrhea from dairy products—adding chocolate to milk can make it easier to digest.

# Jungle Rot

This strawberry-kiwi smoothie feels, looks, and smells like the goop that squishes out of rotting fruit when you walk through a tropical forest.

▸ *Difficulty: Medium* ▸ *Makes 2 servings*

1 kiwi
6 large strawberries, fresh or frozen
½ cup blueberries, fresh or frozen
1 banana
½ cup frozen vanilla yogurt
¾ cup pineapple juice

1. Wash and drain the kiwi, strawberries, and blueberries.
2. Peel the kiwi. Use a blunt knife to cut the kiwi into small pieces.
3. Use a blunt knife to cut the strawberries in half.
4. Peel the banana. Slice it with a blunt knife.
5. Put all the ingredients in a blender. Cover and blend until smooth and slightly frothy.

*For 100 percent authentic jungle rot, use a pomegranate instead of strawberries. Pomegranates have a tough outer skin, so ask an adult to cut it open for you. Then, just scoop out the insides, which look like red fish eggs.*

WORDS to KNOW

**smoothie** a cold drink made with fruit, fruit juice or milk, and either yogurt, ice cream, or sherbet all blended together into a smooth liquid; sometimes other ingredients, such as seeds, nuts, and spices, are added.

What is invisible and smells like a banana?

A monkey fart!

## Putrid Punch

This midnight-black fruit punch with gummy-bug ice cubes is a fun way to gross out your friends' parties!

▶ *Difficulty: Easy*  ▶ *Serves 16 to 20*

32 to 64 gummy bugs (or raisins)
1 package unsweetened grape Kool-Aid
1 package unsweetened orange Kool-Aid
2 cups sugar
3 quarts cold water
1 quart ginger ale

### Step One: Make the Frozen Flies

1. Fill two large ice-cube trays half full with water. Put them in the freezer for several hours, until frozen.
2. Put one or two gummy bugs (or raisins) in each cube.
3. Fill the ice-cube trays the rest of the way with water.
4. Put them in the freezer for several hours, until frozen.

### Step Two: Make the Putrid Punch

1. In a large punch bowl (or pitcher), mix together the Kool-Aid mixes, sugar, and water.
2. Slowly stir in the ginger ale.
3. Add the gummy-bug ice cubes.

*Instead of freezing gummy bugs in the ice cubes, make frozen eyeballs by putting half a green grape with a raisin stuck in the center in each ice cube.*

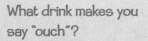

What drink makes you say "ouch"?

Punch!

**FREAKY FOOD FACT:**
Which of these fruits do American kids like best? Write "1" next to the one you guess is the most favorite, "2" next to the second favorite, and so on.

_____Grapes

_____Apples

_____Bananas

_____Berries

_____Peaches

*1. apples 2. bananas 3. grapes*
*4. peaches 5. berries*

# Bottoms Up!

Katy, Joe, and Ivan always clink together their glasses and yell "Bottoms up!" before chugging their favorite drinks in one long gulp. The letters that make up the names of the main flavor in each of their favorite drinks are hidden on their shirts. Rearrange the letters from each shirt to find out who likes which flavor the very best.

The main ingredient in Katy's favorite drink is __ __ __ __.

The main ingredient in Joe's favorite drink is __ __ __ __ __ __ __ __ __.

The main ingredient in Ivan's favorite drink is __ __ __ __ __ __ __ __ __.

# Frozen Flotsam

Make sure you have a teaspoon ready to slurp the gnat-covered flotsam (ice cream with chocolate sprinkles) from this frosty root beer float. Yum!

▸ **Difficulty: Easy**  ▸ **Serves 1**

6 ounces root beer
1 scoop vanilla ice cream
1 teaspoon chocolate cake sprinkles

1. Slowly pour the root beer into a frosted or chilled mug. Fill it part way, leaving about 1 inch from the top. Let stand until the foam goes down.
2. Put a large scoop of ice cream into the mug.
3. Sprinkle the chocolate sprinkles over the top of the ice cream.

*If you don't want to frost the mug or a tall glass, put it in the refrigerator for 5–10 minutes to chill it before adding the sewer water (root beer), flotsam (ice cream), and gnats (chocolate sprinkles).*

Where in school are you most likely to catch a cold?

In the cough-eteria!

CHEF'S SECRET:
To Frost a Mug
Run cool water from the faucet over the outside and inside of a glass or ceramic mug. Put the wet mug in the freezer for 5 to 10 minutes.

# Steaming Coyote Pee

This simple recipe for hot apple cider with cinnamon sticks is the most fun when you tell people it's fresh coyote pee stirred with bark from the tree the coyote peed on.

▶ *Difficulty: Easy*  ▶ *Makes 1 serving*

1 cup apple cider          1 cinnamon stick

1. Pour the apple cider into a microwave-safe mug or cup.
2. Warm the cider in the microwave for about 1 minute, until hot but not bubbling. Let the hot cider sit in the microwave for 10 seconds before removing.
3. Put a cinnamon stick in the cup and serve.

# Hot 'n Chunky Hershey Squirts

This hot chocolate with melting butterscotch chips and mini marshmallows looks a lot like diarrhea. Enjoy!

▶ *Difficulty: Easy*  ▶ *Serves 1*

1 cup milk
2 heaping tablespoons semi-sweet cocoa powder

1 tablespoon butterscotch chips
1 tablespoon mini marshmallows

1. Fill a large microwave-safe mug or cup almost full with milk, leaving about 1 inch from the rim.
2. Heat the milk in the microwave for about 1 minute, until hot but not boiling or curdling. Let the hot chocolate sit in the microwave for 10 seconds before removing.
3. Stir in the butterscotch chips. Top with marshmallows.

*You can leave the cinnamon stick in the mug while you sip the hot pee or you can remove it before you drink.*

**FREAKY FOOD FACT:**
Curds Away!
What type of milk never curdles?
**A.** Cow milk
**B.** Goat milk
**C.** Camel milk
**D.** Human milk

*C. Camel milk!*

*You can substitute water and instant hot chocolate mix for the milk and cocoa powder if you'd like, or you can use chocolate syrup instead of cocoa powder.*

# Gag Me with a Spoonerism

A spoonerism is when the letters or syllables in words or phrases get flip-flopped and form a silly phrase. For example, "This is the pun fart" is a spoonerism for "This is the fun part."

The word "spoonerism" is named after William Archibald Spooner, a professor in England more than seventy years ago who was famous for accidentally goofing up his words—for instance, saying, "Having tasted two worms," when he meant to say, "Having wasted two terms." Try to figure out the real words for these spoonerisms. (Hint: They're all food terms.)

1. dot hog          ___ ___
2. brown fudgie     _____ _____
3. chilled grease   _____ _____
4. chork pops       _____ _____
5. chalk hock a lot ___ _____
6. sea poop         ___ ____
7. toot farts       _____ _____
8. belly jeans      _____ _____
9. snail tracks     _____ _____
10. nasal hut       _____

# Chapter 9

# Gross Gags and Fun Stuff

## Fake Barf

You can actually eat this fake barf—if you can stomach the thought of it.

▶ **Difficulty: Hard**   ▶ **Makes 1 blob of barf**

¼ cup applesauce
1 envelope (¼ ounce) unflavored gelatin
⅛ teaspoon cocoa powder
½ cup uncooked oatmeal
Raisin bran cereal (about ½ cup)
Handful of raisins
Cooking oil spray

1. Warm the applesauce in the frying pan over low heat, stirring constantly, just until heated through.
2. Stir in the gelatin and cocoa powder. Remove from heat.
3. Sprinkle a handful of oatmeal over the applesauce mixture. Stir it in just enough to mix the ingredients. The mixture should be lumpy and sticky.
4. Stir a handful of raisin bran into the oatmeal mixture, just enough to mix it in.
5. Add more oatmeal and raisin bran, a little at a time, until the mixture has the look and consistency of vomit.
6. Spray a dinner plate with cooking oil.
7. Spread the oatmeal mixture on the plate. Use a spoon or your hands to mold it into the shape of a pile of puke.
8. Scatter a small handful of raisins on the gooey gunk.
9. Let the barf sit for a few hours to cool and to set.

*When you're ready to put the fake barf somewhere for one of your family members to discover, use a spatula to remove it from the plate.*

**WORDS to KNOW**

**edible** anything that is safe to eat—even if it looks disgusting, smells awful, and tastes nasty

What's worse than finding a worm in your half-eaten apple?

Finding half a worm!

# Nasty Nibbles

Do you know this little ditty? *Everybody's doing it, doing it, doing it / Picking their nose and chewing it, chewing it / Thinking it's candy, when it's not / It's s-n-o-t, snot, snot, snot!* Well, maybe not everybody eats snot, but some people do. Guess what? That's not the only yucky stuff people eat that is not meant to be eaten. Write the letter that goes with the number to find out the other disgusting things some people eat.

__ __ __ __ __ __ __
2  15  15  7  5  17  18

__ __ __ __ __ __ __ __ __ __
6  9  14  7  5  17  14  1  9  12  18

__ __ __ __ __
18  3  1  2  18

__ __ __ __ __ __ __ __
4  5  1  4  18  11  9  14

__ __ __ __
8  1  9  17

__ __ __ __
18  14  15  19

__ __ __ __ __ __
19  15  5  10  1  13

__ __ __ __ __ __
5  1  17  21  1  22

__ __ __ __ __
2  12  15  15  4

__ __ __ __ __ __ __ __ __
14  1  20  5  12  12  9  14  19

| 1 = a |
| 2 = b |
| 3 = c |
| 4 = d |
| 5 = e |
| 6 = f |
| 7 = g |
| 8 = h |
| 9 = i |
| 10 = j |
| 11 = k |
| 12 = l |
| 13 = m |
| 14 = n |
| 15 = o |
| 16 = p |
| 17 = r |
| 18 = s |
| 19 = t |
| 20 = v |
| 21 = w |
| 22 = x |

## Fake Boogers and Snot

You can smear this edible nose blow on your hand in secret, pretend sneeze in front of your family or friends, and then lick the fake boogers and snot off your hand.

▶ *Difficulty: Easy*  ▶ *Makes about 8 fake nose blows*

½ cup water
3 (¼-ounce) envelopes unflavored gelatin
⅓ to ½ cup light corn syrup
A few white raisins

1. Put the water in a microwave-safe cup or mug. Heat just until it starts to boil.
2. Sprinkle the gelatin into the hot water. Stir with a fork to dissolve the gelatin. Let it set for a few minutes, until it sets to a loose gel.
3. Add enough corn syrup to make 1 cup. Stir with a fork to mix.
4. Add a small handful of white raisins.
5. If the goop thickens too much, add hot water by the teaspoon until it's loose enough to lift with a fork.

🐛 *Use immediately, lifting the booger-covered snot out of the cup with a fork.*

**FREAKY FOOD FACT:**
Record-Breaking Nose Blow
The world's record for the longest strand of spaghetti blown out of a person's nose is 7½ feet. Don't try this at home, or at school, or in restaurants, or at Grandma's, or anywhere!

# Fake Slime

This slimy green gunk is not edible. Make it for fun and gags only—not for eating!

▸ *Difficulty: Medium*  ▸ *Makes about 2½ cups*

⅛ cup borax laundry booster
2 cups plus ¼ cup water
¼ cup white glue (such as Elmer's)
1 or 2 drops green food coloring

## WORDS to KNOW

**knead** to repeatedly fold, press, and turn a mixture of ingredients, called "dough" or "batter," until it is smooth and pliable like putty

1. In a small saucepan, mix together the borax and 2 cups of water.
2. Stirring constantly, heat over a medium burner until the borax dissolves completely. Remove from heat and set aside to cool.
3. In a small cup, mix together the glue and the remaining ¼ cup of water.
4. Put a plastic food storage bag that seals inside a large plastic drinking glass. Fold the open sides of the bag over the rim of the glass.
5. Pour (or scrape) the glue mixture into the bag.
6. Stir the food coloring into the borax mixture.
7. Pour the borax mixture into the plastic bag.
8. Close the bag, squeezing out as much air as possible.
9. Knead the mixture in the closed bag until it forms into slime. Squeeze the slime into a plastic container with a tight-fitting lid. This makes it easier to use and to store any leftovers. An empty, clean, and dry margarine tub works well for this.

🐛 *Make sure not to get the slime on furniture, carpet, clothing, or walls because the food coloring will stain.*

## Fake Wounds

It's fun to show off your fake wound to friends—and to freak out your mom! Just remember: These are not edible.

▸ *Difficulty: Hard*  ▸ *Makes 1 fake wound*

1 tablespoon (finger full) petroleum jelly
3 or 4 drops red food coloring
2 to 3 pinches cocoa powder
1 white tissue

1. Put a tablespoon of petroleum jelly into a small bowl.
2. Stir in 3 drops of food coloring. If it isn't red enough, add another drop of food coloring.
3. Stir in a pinch of cocoa powder to darken the red to the color of real blood.
4. Rip off a small rectangle of tissue, about 3 inches by 2 inches.
5. Place the rectangle of tissue on your arm or wherever you want your wound to be.
6. Cover the tissue with the blood-red petroleum jelly.
7. Use your fingers to shape the petroleum jelly to look like a wound site—a small mound that's slightly higher in the center.
8. Smear the blood-red petroleum jelly on the center of the wound.
9. Sprinkle cocoa on the edges of the wound and use your finger to rub in the cocoa a little.

🐌 *If you want to cover yourself with several oozing wounds, just use a bigger bowl and double, triple, or even quadruple the recipe.*

What do you get if you cross a snake with a pie?

A pie-thon!

# Finger Paint

This inedible (but nontoxic) finger paint gives you double the fun: First, when you stick your fingers in the slimy goop and spread it on the page, and again when you see the repulsed looks on your family's faces when you show them the yucky pictures you drew!

▶ *Difficulty: Medium*   ▶ *Makes 5 small jars of finger paint*

1 cup cold water, divided into ¾ cup and ¼ cup
½ cup cornstarch
1 (3-ounce) envelope unflavored gelatin
½ cup Ivory soap flakes or laundry detergent
Food coloring, 5 colors

1. Put ¼ cup of cold water in a small bowl. Add the gelatin to water in the bowl. Let stand for several minutes.
2. Put ¾ cup of cold water in a saucepan. Add the cornstarch to the saucepan. Stir with a fork until the cornstarch is dissolved.
3. Cook the cornstarch and water over medium heat, stirring constantly, until it is clear and starts to boil. Remove from heat.
4. Add the softened gelatin to the hot starchy water. Stir gently and slowly to fold in. Add the soap and stir until dissolved. Let cool.
5. Divide the cooled water mixture into 5 small jars or plastic bowls.
6. Put a different color of food coloring in each jar and stir to mix. Start with 2 drops and then add more drops one at a time until you get the color you want.
7. Store leftover finger paint in glass or plastic containers with tight-fitting lids. Note: Finger paint will stain fabric, plastic, and other materials.

**FREAKY FOOD FACT:**
Legume Ka-Boom!
Peanuts are used to manufacture dynamite.

You can mix different colors together to create your own gross colors of finger paint—for example, Poop Brown (red and green), Snot Green (green and yellow), and Rot-Gut Black (red, green, blue).

## Smelly Play Dough

You can make this play dough with any flavor of Kool-Aid and shape it into gross stuff like pig's brains, elephant dung, pimple faces, and pointy-tongued lizards.

▶ *Difficulty: Hard* ▶ *Makes 1 tub of play dough*

1 cup cold water
1 tablespoon vegetable oil
2 packages of same flavor of unsweetened Kool-Aid (or similar drink mix)
¼ cup salt
1 cup flour
5 teaspoons cream of tartar

1. In a medium saucepan, combine water, oil, Kool-Aid, and salt.
2. Cook over medium heat and stir until the salt dissolves.
3. Add the flour and cream of tartar in the saucepan all at once.
4. Continue cooking and stirring for a few minutes, until the dough is mixed very well and forms a ball. Remove from the heat immediately (as soon as it forms a ball).
5. Dump onto an ungreased cookie sheet. Let the dough cool enough for you to handle it comfortably.
6. While the dough is still warm, knead it for a few minutes, until it is smooth and pliable.
7. Let the dough finish cooling completely, to room temperature, before shaping it into hideously gross stuff.

*Instead of using two packages of the same flavor of Kool-Aid, you can experiment with combining different flavors to come up with play dough with disgusting colors and sickening smells.*

CHEF'S SECRET:
Save It for a Rainy Day
Store your play dough in a resealable plastic bag or in a plastic container with a lid (such as a clean margarine tub) to keep it fresh and pliable.

# Slimed!

If you can find your way from the sponge to the end before their mom slips and falls on it, maybe Megan and Todd won't get in deep doo-doo for having a slime fight in the house! On your sponge, get slimed, and go!

# Raunchy Food Trivia

As you solve this crossword you'll discover a bunch of fun and funky things about food that are sure to gross you out!

## Down

1. Pork rinds are made from this part of a hog. (Clue: Rhymes with "chin.")
2. This can happen if your stomach "turns" when you eat or smell rotten food.
3. The common name for curdled soy bean (a.k.a. "bean crud"), which is a source of protein for vegetarians.
4. A red, heart-shaped fruit with seeds on its skin that look like zits, often eaten with shortcake and whipped cream.
5. Indians of the rainforest in Brazil eat omelets made from the eggs of this big, hairy creature.
6. This deep-fried delicacy is popular in France, but Kermit says his are made for hopping.
7. These sandwiches are made with marshmallow, chocolate, and graham crackers.
9. "Lubberwort" is another name for _____ food. (Clue: Rhymes with "gunk.")
10. Before the Civil War, people in the South called these "monkey nuts" and "goober peas."
13. These grow in bunches on a vine and are red, green, or purple when ripe. When these fruits are dried and shriveled up, they're called "raisins."
14. This small, red, bitter fruit is nicknamed "bounce berry" because it bounces if dropped on the ground. (Clue: Often served on Thanksgiving.)
17. A dry, yellowish-white cheese that "farts" while it is aging, causing holes to form in the cheese when the gas bubbles up and bursts.
19. It takes 4 tons of dried up grapes to produce 1 ton of these chewy fruits.
21. Animal intestines give these deli meats their turd-like shape. (Clue: They're usually served in buns or mixed with baked beans.)
22. Inuits (Eskimos) eat a special dish they call "stinky tail," which is made from the fermented tail of this buck-toothed, paddle-tailed, water-loving, dam-building animal.
24. A kind of jam you don't want to eat, because it usually smells like dirty feet.

## Across

2. This main ingredient in PB&J sandwiches is also good for removing chewing gum from hair and clothes.
4. Herring is a small and _____ fish. (Clue: You might need to hold your nose to eat it.)
5. Fungi that are sniffed out by pigs. It's also the name of a fancy chocolate candy with a creamy center.
8. The letters of this canned meat product stand for shoulder, pork, ham. It's also the name of e-mail you don't want.
10. "Chitlins" (or "chitterlings") are a Southern dish made with onions, hot peppers, vinegar, and the intestines of this animal. (Clue: Oink!)
11. A yellow fruit that can be split and that monkeys love.
12. These are hatched by chickens, and they smell like sulfur when they're rotten.
13. An ingredient commonly found in Italian food that has the nickname "stinky rose."
15. This often happens when you eat a lot of spicy food or beans.
16. "Escargot" is a fancy word for these disgusting critters, cooked in garlic and oil or butter. (Clue: They slither on the ground and leave a trail of slime behind them.)
18. This often happens when you drink soda really fast.
20. "Calamari" is a fancy name for this cooked sea creature. (Clue: Rhymes with "skid," as in the skid marks on underwear.)
23. Eighty percent of the people in the world eat these types of small, crawling, and flying critters.
25. Seventy out of 100 people pick their noses, and 3 out of those 70 nose-pickers eat these.
26. This is what you get when you eat way too many prunes. (Clue: There's a song about it in Chapter 5.)

# Gastronomical Glossary

Several important cooking terms are explained in Chapter 1. You'll also find several terms explained in the Words to Know boxes scattered throughout the book. To make it easy as pie to look up the meaning of all the words you'll need to know while preparing the recipes in this book, they're all here in one place and in alphabetical order. By the way, gastronomical means "having to do with good eating," and a glossary is a mini dictionary that defines special words used in a book.

**al dente**—an Italian word that means "to the tooth;" cooking pasta until it is tender but still firm and gives a slight resistance when you bite into it

**Alfredo sauce**—a white sauce made of butter, cream, and Parmesan cheese, served over pasta

**au gratin**—covered with bread crumbs and/or butter and grated cheese and browned in the oven

**bake**—to cook something inside the oven, using the heat from the bottom of the oven

**baking pan**—a glass or metal pan used for cooking food in the oven; can be square or rectangular and is usually shallow (not very deep)

**batter**—a soft and wet mixture of ingredients, such as sugar, eggs, flour, spices, butter, and milk, that is used to cook or bake many different things, including cakes, cookies, the coating on fried foods, muffins, and pancakes

**beat**—to mix ingredients together fast and hard with an electric mixer, fork, spoon, or whisk

**blend**—to mix ingredients together to form a smooth batter, dough, or liquid

**blender**—an electric appliance used for blending, chopping, grinding, and mixing foods; it has a glass or metal pitcher with a tight-fitting lid attached to it

**boil**—to heat a liquid or to cook solid food in a liquid until the liquid bubbles; some recipes call for a "full boil," which means the liquid is bubbly all over, while other recipes say to heat the liquid until it "starts" to boil, which means only until small bubbles begin to form

**boil over**—when boiling liquid rises above the top edge of the pot and falls over the sides of the pot

**blunt knife**—a knife with a dull edge, rather than a sharp edge, such as a butter knife; some blunt knives have a serrated edge, which helps in cutting bread and many other solid foods

**broil**—to cook food under the broiler part of the oven where the heat comes from the top; a broiler is either part of an oven or is its own separate unit

**brown**—to cook food on the stovetop or to bake in the oven until the food turns brown and crispy on the outside

**can opener**—an electric appliance or a manual tool used to open metal cans containing food

**caramelize**—heating sugar or food covered in a sugary ingredient (such as brown sugar or maple syrup) until it melts and turns the color and constancy of caramel candy

# Gastronomical Glossary

**casserole dish**—a large glass dish with sides that is used to make casseroles and baked foods in the oven; available in round, oval, square, and rectangular shapes and in different sizes (usually 1-quart or 2-quart), and they often have lids

**chill**—to put ingredients, mixtures, or prepared food in a refrigerator until it is cold

**chop**—to cut food into small pieces with a blender, knife, or food processor

**colander**—a large bowl with holes in it used to drain water or liquid from foods such as vegetables, boiled potatoes, and cooked pasta; can be metal or plastic, and usually has a small handle on each side

**confectioners' sugar**—sugar that has been ground to a fine powder and mixed with cornstarch, which causes the food being prepared to thicken (such as with cake frosting)

**cookie sheet**—a flat metal sheet used for baking cookies and many other solid foods; sometimes called a "baking sheet"

**cooking oil spray**—a vegetable oil that comes in a spray can, used to grease pots and other cooking ware; also sometimes sprayed directly on foods to help brown them during baking or broiling.

**cooking spoon**—a large spoon (made of metal, hard plastic, or wood) with a long handle; some cooking spoons have slats or holes in them

**cool**—to let food sit at room temperature until it is no longer hot

**core**—to remove the center of a fruit or vegetable containing the seeds, leaving the outer skin and enough flesh for the fruit to maintain its shape; the center of a vegetable or fruit (such as an apple)

**cream**—to mix wet and dry ingredients together (such as butter, eggs, sugar, and flour) until they form a smooth and creamy mixture

**cutting board**—a flat board made of wood, hard plastic, or glass used to cut food on

**delicacy**—a special food that a group of people really like

**dice**—to cut food into very small, even-sized, square-shaped pieces

**drain**—to pour off the liquid in which food is stored or cooked, usually by pouring the food into a colander

**drizzle**—to sprinkle a liquid ingredient, such as chocolate sauce or melted butter, over a food

**dry mixture**—a combination of certain dry ingredients in a recipe—such as flour, baking soda, baking powder, salt, and dried herbs and spices

**Dutch oven**—a large, heavy pot with a tight-fitting lid that is shaped like a dome

**edible**—can be eaten

**electric mixer**—an electric appliance used for mixing ingredients

**entrée**—the main course of a meal, such as spaghetti with meat balls

**fold**—to combine ingredients by gently and repeatedly turning the mixture over just until the different foods are mixed together

**fondue**—bite-sized foods (bread, meat, poultry, fish, fruit, or vegetables) skewered on a long, thin metal fork and dipped in melted cheese, melted chocolate, hot oil, broth, or a sauce

**frappe**—a blended drink that is frozen or partially frozen so that it's slushy and has foam on top

**fry**—to cook food in fat or oil in a skillet over medium to high heat

**gel**—to allow a liquid to set or firm up (congeal) to the consistency of jelly

**glass measuring cup**—a glass cup with a handle, a spout, and measurements printed on the side of the cup, used to measure liquids; comes in 1-cup, 2-cup, and 4-cup sizes

**grate**—to shred food into very tiny pieces with a shredder, blender, or food processor

**grease**—to spray or spread a thin layer of butter, margarine, shortening, or oil on a baking pan or dish to prevent food from sticking

**griddle**—a flat, square pan used to grill pancakes, French toast, sandwiches, hamburgers, and other food

**ice-cream scoop**—a hard plastic or metal tool shaped like either a giant spoon or a round ball, used to scoop ice cream and sherbet out of the carton; can also be used to scoop cookie batter, sour cream, and other foods

**knead**—to repeatedly fold, punch, press, and turn dough or batter to work air into it and to make it the right consistency—for example, to make bread dough smooth and pliable, like silly putty

**knife**—a tool with a handle and a flat, sharp edge, used for cutting, slicing, or carving food; available in many sizes, and some have serrated edges

**ladle**—a deep, rounded spoon with a long handle used to scoop sauces, soups, and other liquids out of a pot, serving dish, or other container

**level**—a measuring cup or spoon filled with a dry ingredient that is then flattened with a blunt knife so that the top of an ingredient is not overflowing or "rounded"

**measuring cups**—metal or plastic cups of many different sizes (⅛ cup, ¼ cup, ⅓ cup, ¾ cup, and 1 cup) used to measure dry ingredients, usually nested so the smaller ones fit inside the larger ones to form a single stack of cups

**microwave oven**—an electrical appliance that looks like a small oven but is used to warm, cook, melt, and boil food; cooks food very quickly using electromagnetic waves (microwaves)

**mince**—to cut food into tiny pieces using a knife, grater, or food processor

**mix**—to stir together two or more ingredients to combine them

**mixing bowls**—deep bowls of varying widths and made of glass or metal, used to blend, mix, or whip ingredients together.

**muffin tins**—a baking pan with small, rounded cups used for baking cupcakes and muffins, usually made of metal and sometimes out of glass

**new potatoes**—very small potatoes that are harvested early, before they can grow large; sometimes called "young" or "baby" potatoes, they have a thinner skin and their flesh is sweeter and firmer than mature potatoes

**oven**—an electric or gas appliance used for baking and broiling food

**oven mitts**—large, thick mittens made of fire-resistant material, used to handle hot pots and pans, cooking utensils, and other cookware

**parchment paper**—strong, see-through paper that can withstand heat and is used to wrap foods in to seal in juices and flavors while baking

**pastry brush**—a small brush used to spread melted butter and sauces over food

**pie plate**—a shallow dish made of glass or metal, used for baking pies and other baked goods; sometimes called a "pie tin" or "pie pan"

**peel**—to remove skin from fruits and vegetables

**pitcher**—A large glass, plastic, or metal container with a handle and a spout used for serving water or cold drinks

**pitted**—when the seed in the center of the fruit is removed—such as with apricots, avocados, peaches, and olives

**pizza cutter**—a tool with a handle on one end and a thin, sharp wheel at the other end used to cut pizza, cookie dough, bread dough, and other mushy foods

**plate**—a small, flat dish used to serve individual helpings of food

**platter**—a large, flat dish used to serve food "family style," from which individual servings are dished out at the table

**potato masher**—a tool used to mash cooked potatoes or soft foods, such as avocados, until they are smooth

**pot holders**—thick, fire-resistant material, usually in the shape of a square, used to handle hot pots and pans, cooking utensils, and other cookware

**preheat**—to turn on a cooking appliance (such as an oven, an electric skillet, or an electric crock pot), set it to the desired temperature, and wait until it reaches that temperature before putting the food in to cook; oil and liquids are also sometimes preheated in a pan on a stovetop burner

**puree**—to mix and mash food until it is the consistency of baby food (or baby poop)

**rolling pin**—a roller made of wood, plastic, or marble with handles on each end, used to flatten dough such as for piecrust, biscuits, and cookies

**rounded**—a measuring cup or spoon filled until the ingredient makes a slight mound on top, rather than being "level"

**rubber spatula**—a tool with a flat rubber tip and a long handle, used to remove batter or liquids from a blender, food processor, or mixing bowl and to spread or level foods, such as icing on a cake and brownie batter in a pan

**saucepan**—a pot with a long handle used to cook food on a stovetop; come in several sizes, often with form-fitting lids

**sauté**—to cook food on a low to medium temperature in a skillet with a small amount of butter, margarine, or oil

**serrated knife**—a sharp knife that has an edge with a row of small notches that are similar to the teeth on a saw

**serving bowls**—different sizes and shapes of bowls, usually made of glass but sometimes made of plastic or wood, used to serve food "family style" by dishing out individual helpings at the table.

**set**—to let prepared food, such as brownies and pudding, sit or cool without stirring until it congeals (firms up) to the desired consistency

**shish kabob**—cubes of marinated meat and sometimes vegetables cooked on a skewer (stick) over hot coals or broiled

**shred**—to cut food into small, thin strips, using a shredder, blender, or food processor

**simmer**—to cook food over low heat, allowing it to bubble gently but not boil fully

**skewer**—a long, thin stick made of wood or metal, used to cook shish kabobs

**skillet**—a shallow pan used for frying, stir-frying, and sautéing food in hot fat or oil

**slice**—to cut food into thin slices of about the same size, such as with bread

**smoothie**—a cold drink made with fruit, fruit juice or milk, and either yogurt, ice cream, or sherbet all blended together into a smooth liquid; sometimes other ingredients such as seeds, nuts, and spices are added

**spatula**—a tool with a flat metal shovel on one end and a long handle on the other, used to flip, lift, turn, and remove foods (such as cookies, eggs, grilled cheese sandwiches, hamburgers, and pancakes) from pots, pans, and other cookware

**spritzer**—fruit juice mixed with carbonated (bubbly) water or flavored soda, such as ginger ale

**steam**—to cook food over boiling water so the steam (not the water) cooks the food

**stir**—to turn food in a circular motion with a spoon

**stir-fry**—to cook food in a small amount of oil in a wok or skillet over high heat while stirring continuously

**stock**—a liquid broth made from slowly cooking meat, bones, and/or vegetables in water over low heat; also called "soup stock" or "soup base"

**stove**—an electric or gas appliance with burners for cooking food, also called a "range" (A stove or range may have only a stovetop and no oven, or it can be a stovetop and oven combined.)

**taco**—a small tortilla that is folded, filled with ingredients (such as meat, cheese, lettuce), and prepared soft (warmed) or crisp (fried)

**thicken**—to heat and stir a combination of water, milk, broth, and sometimes butter or margarine with a thickening agent such as flour or cornstarch until the mixture turns from liquid to a heavy sauce, such as gravy, or a soft solid, such as pudding

**toast**—to cook food, such as bread, coconut, and nuts, in a toaster or oven until the surface turns crispy and golden brown

**toaster**—an electric appliance with two or four slots, used to toast bread, English muffins, and bagels

**tongs**—a metal tool with a long handle and rounded pinchers at the other end (for grabbing food)

**tortilla**—a flat, round, thin bread made from wheat flour or cornmeal; usually filled or topped with other ingredients and served flat (quesadilla), wrapped (burrito), rolled up (enchilada), or folded (taco)

**utensils**—a variety of hand-held tools used to prepare and cook food

**vegetable peeler**—a tool with a handle on one end and a sharp implement that looks like a long keyhole on the other, used to scrape the skin off of apples, carrots, cucumbers, pears, potatoes, zucchini, and other vegetables; sometimes called a "potato peeler"

**wet mixture**—a combination of certain wet ingredients in a recipe—such as butter, shortening, oil, water, milk, eggs, sugar, brown sugar, syrup, and liquid extracts

**whip**—to beat food rapidly with a blender, eggbeater, electric mixer, food processor, fork, or whisk.

**whisk**—a tool used to combine ingredients and to beat foods rapidly

**wok**—a wide and deep pan with a rounded bottom used to stir-fry food in a small amount of very hot oil

**wooden spoons**—long-handled spoons made out of wood and in many different sizes, used for mixing and stirring all types of food

# Puzzle Answers

page vi • Appliance Monsters

page 3 • Tool Mess!

page 16 • Trouble at the Table
*Tina told Tony not to taste toenails at the table.*

page 28 • Can You Say Flatulence?

page 33 •
Race to the Latrine

# Puzzle Answers

**page 44** • Barf-A-Rhyme

| | |
|---|---|
| scarf . . . . . . barf | duke . . . . . . puke |
| comet . . . . . vomit | shelf . . . . . . ralph |
| twirl. . . . . . . hurl | use hunch . . lose lunch |
| snow . . . . . . blow | fetch . . . . . . retch |
| woodchuck. . upchuck | chin up . . . . throw up |
| sleeve . . . . . heave | hesitate . . . . regurgitate |

**page 51** • Eewwww! Who Eats This Stuff?

Baked rooster combs . . . . . . . . . Italy
Beef blood pudding . . . . . . . . . . Norway
Bird's nest soup. . . . . . . . . . . . . China
Blubber . . . . . . . . . . . . . . . . . . The Arctic
Boiled fish eyes . . . . . . . . . . . . The Philippines
Broiled beetle grubs. . . . . . . . . Japan
Deep-fried monkey toes . . . . . . Indonesia
Fried squirrel brain. . . . . . . . . . United States (Southern)
Raw turtle eggs . . . . . . . . . . . . Nicaragua
Roasted bat. . . . . . . . . . . . . . . Samoa
Salted, sun-dried grasshoppers. . . Mexico
Sautéed camel's feet . . . . . . . France
Spoiled yak milk. . . . . . . . . . . Tibet
Warm cow urine. . . . . . . . . . . Kenya
White ant pie . . . . . . . . . . . . . Tanzania

**page 71** •
Slurp-ghetti

**page 76** • Find and Sing

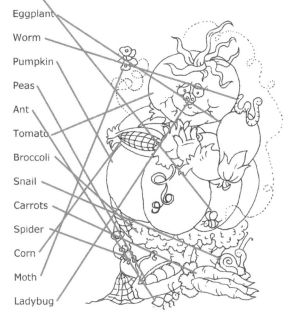

**page 56** •
Funky Fridge

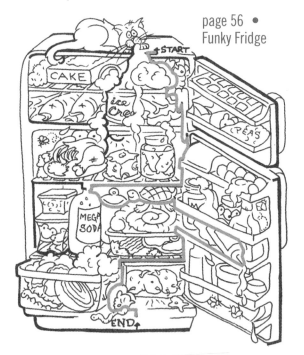

**page 87** • Bug-Eating Veggie Ogress

Bee
Eggplant
Worm
Pumpkin
Peas
Ant
Tomato
Broccoli
Snail
Carrots
Spider
Corn
Moth
Ladybug

# Puzzle Answers

**page 92 • Poo-ey!**

| | |
|---|---|
| vinegar | moldy bread |
| Brussels sprouts | rotten eggs |
| blue cheese | spoiled milk |
| tuna fish | rancid meat |

**page 106 • Eat Dirt!**

**page 113 • Bottoms Up!**

Kate = lime, Joe = raspberry, Ivan = chocolate.

**page 116 • Gag Me with a Spoonerism**

1. dot hog . . . . . . . . hot dog
2. brown fudgie . . . . fudge brownie
3. chilled grease . . . grilled cheese
4. chork pops . . . . . pork chops
5. chalk hock a lot . . hot chocolate
6. sea poop . . . . . . . pea soup
7. toot farts . . . . . . . fruit tarts
8. belly jeans . . . . . . jelly beans
9. snail tracks . . . . . trail snacks
10. nasal hut . . . . . . . hazelnut

**page 119 •**

Nasty Nibbles

(A) boogers
(B) fingernails
(C) scabs
(D) dead skin
(E) hair
(F) snot
(G) toe jam
(H) ear wax
(I) blood
(J) navel lint

**page 125 •**

Slimed!

**page 127 • Raunchy Food Trivia**

# The Everything® **KIDS'** Series!

Packed with tons of information, activities, and puzzles, the Everything® Kids' books are perennial bestsellers that keep kids active and engaged.

Each book is two-color, 8" x 9¼", and 144 pages.

The Everything® Kids' Presidents Book
1-59869-262-3, $7.95

The Everything® Kids' States Book
1-59869-263-1, $7.95

A silly, goofy, and undeniably icky addition to
the Everything® Kids' series . . .

# The Everything® Kids'
## GROSS
### Series

Chock–full of sickening entertainment for hours of disgusting fun.

The Everything® Kids'
Gross Jokes Book
1-59337-448-8, $7.95

The Everything® Kids'
Gross Cookbook
1-59869-324-7, $7.95

The Everything® Kids' Gross
Puzzle & Activity Book
1-59337-447-X, $7.95

The Everything® Kids'
Gross Mazes Book
1-59337-616-2, $7.95

The Everything® Kids' Gross
Hidden Pictures Book
1-59337-615-4, $7.95

# Other Everything® Kids' Titles Available

The Everything® Kids' Animal Puzzle & Activity Book
1-59337-305-8

The Everything® Kids' Baseball Book, 4th Ed.
1-59337-614-6

The Everything® Kids' Bible Trivia Book
1-59337-031-8

The Everything® Kids' Bugs Book
1-58062-892-3

The Everything® Kids' Cars and Trucks
Puzzle & Activity Book
1-59337-703-7

The Everything® Kids' Christmas Puzzle
& Activity Book
1-58062-965-2

The Everything® Kids' Cookbook
1-58062-658-0

The Everything® Kids' Crazy Puzzles Book
1-59337-361-9

The Everything® Kids' Dinosaurs Book
1-59337-360-0

The Everything® Kids' First Spanish Puzzle & Activity Book
1-59337-717-7

The Everything® Kids' Halloween Puzzle &
Activity Book
1-58062-959-8

The Everything® Kids' Hidden Pictures Book
1-59337-128-4

The Everything® Kids' Horses Book
1-59337-608-1

The Everything® Kids' Joke Book
1-58062-686-6

The Everything® Kids' Knock Knock Book
1-59337-127-6

The Everything® Kids' Learning Spanish Book
1-59337-716-9

The Everything® Kids' Math Puzzles Book
1-58062-773-0

The Everything® Kids' Mazes Book
1-58062-558-4

The Everything® Kids' Money Book
1-58062-685-8

The Everything® Kids' Nature Book
1-58062-684-X

The Everything® Kids' Pirates Puzzle and Activity Book
1-59337-607-3

The Everything® Kids' Princess Puzzle & Activity Book
1-59337-704-5

The Everything® Kids' Puzzle Book
1-58062-687-4

The Everything® Kids' Riddles & Brain Teasers Book
1-59337-036-9

The Everything® Kids' Science Experiments Book
1-58062-557-6

The Everything® Kids' Sharks Book
1-59337-304-X

The Everything® Kids' Soccer Book
1-58062-642-4

The Everything® Kids' Travel Activity Book
1-58062-641-6